A Game Called Survival

By the same author

Prisoner At Large

Joan Knights
1980.

A Game Called Survival

The story of Betty di San Marzano and her children in wartime Italy

Ian Reid

Evans

Evans Brothers Limited London

Published by Evans Brothers Limited
Montague House, Russell Square
London, WC1B 5BX

First published 1980

Jacket illustration by Alexa Rutherford

British Library Cataloguing in Publication Data
Reid, Ian, *b. 1915*
A game called survival.
1. San Marzano, Betty, contessa di
2. Antifascists – Italy
I. Title
940.53'45 DG575.S/

ISBN 0–237–45527–7

Phototypeset in Great Britain by
Filmtype Services Limited, Scarborough

Printed in Great Britain by
Redwood Burn Limited,
Trowbridge & Esher

PRA 6846

Contents

Illustrations

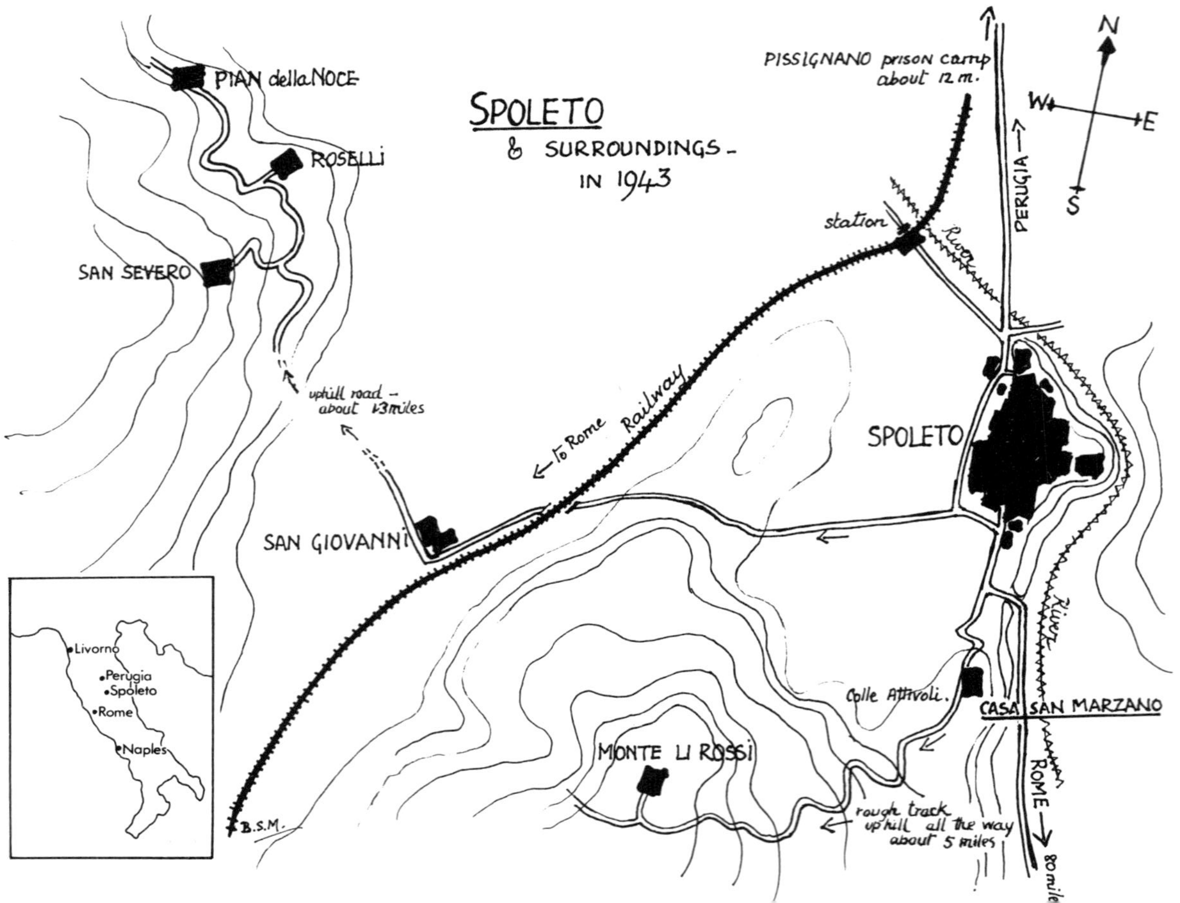

SPOLETO
& SURROUNDINGS -
IN 1943
PIAN della NOCE
ROSELLI
SAN SEVERO
uphill road -
about 1/3 miles
SAN GIOVANNI
← To Rome
Railway
B.S.M.
PISSIGNANO prison camp
about 12 m.
N
W
E
S
PERUGIA →
station
River
SPOLETO
River
Colle Attivoli.
CASA SAN MARZANO
MONTE LI ROSSI
rough track
uphill all the way
about 5 miles
ROME →
80 mile
Livorno
Perugia
Spoleto
Rome
Naples

Note on the Rome-Berlin Axis

The story of Betty di San Marzano and her children begins in September 1943. Since June 1940, Italy had been fighting on the side of Germany, and a brief note on her involvement in the Second World War may be useful. To readers who would like to study this period in greater detail I strongly recommend Christopher Hibbert's excellent biography, *Benito Mussolini, The Rise and Fall of il Duce*, on which I have drawn heavily for this note and for dates throughout the book.

On 10 June 1940, from the balcony overlooking Piazza Venezia in Rome, Mussolini proclaimed that the Italians were 'entering the lists against the plutocratic and reactionary democracies of the West, who have always hindered the advance and often plotted against the very existence of the Italian people'.

His promise 'to conquer' and finally to give 'a long period of peace with justice to Italy, to Europe, and to the world' never looked likely to be fulfilled. From the first the war went badly for Italy which, despite huge State expenditure for military purposes, was, as Christopher Hibbert points out, 'shamefully ill equipped to conduct a major war'.

The plotting against Mussolini, at first limited to secret contacts between the Royal Court and some officers of the General Staff, had begun as early as November 1942, after General Montgomery's victory at El Alamein. By the spring of 1943 all the Axis forces in North Africa had been defeated, and on 10 July 1943 the Allies invaded Sicily.

On 23 July a dramatic meeting of the Grand Council of Fascism which lasted until the small hours of the next morning finally approved a resolution moved by Count Dino Grandi virtually calling for Mussolini's resignation. After an audience with King Victor Emmanuel III on 25 July Mussolini was arrested.

As Head of Government to replace him the King appointed Marshal

Pietro Badoglio who, however, proclaimed after the announcement of Mussolini's resignation that the war would go on and that Italy would remain true to her Allies. With the Germans still in Rome and the German Army still in control of most of Italy, Badoglio had little choice.

After the Allied landing in the south of Italy, however, in early September the King and Badoglio's Government fled from Rome to Pescara and then to Brindisi, and on 8 September 1943 Badoglio announced that Italy had concluded an Armistice with the Allies and was no longer in the war.

Preface

Betty, Contessa di San Marzano, is the daughter of Colonel Clarence Johnson, late Bengal Lancers. Her Australian mother came from an old Melbourne family called Brodribb – there is a small village and a river of that name. She was first cousin to Richard Casey, who, as Lord Casey, was Governor-General of Australia from 1965 to 1969.

Betty spent her early childhood near Melbourne where her father, retired from the Indian Army, was growing apples. On the outbreak of the First World War Colonel Johnson joined the Australian army, went with them to Gallipoli, was wounded and sent to England. Mrs Johnson therefore gathered up her two children and, braving the 1915 U-boat menace, undertook the hazardous voyage from Australia to Britain.

Colonel Johnson was a compulsive traveller, and in 1926, living in London with his family, he announced his intention of emigrating to British Columbia. Betty, by then a dedicated art student, was appalled and refused to accompany her parents, at least until she had been allowed to see the art treasures of Rome. Her father eventually gave in, and they arrived in the Eternal City for a four-month stay on 1 January 1927.

One of their letters of introduction was to a Mrs Mussa, the English wife of an Italian Colonel, who invited them to *thé dansants*, all the rage in Rome as well as in London at the time. As an escort for the Johnsons' daughter Colonel Mussa offered to bring one of his young officers, Conte Valentino Asinari di San Marzano, whose father was the General commanding the Carabinieri.

It was a case of love at first sight. Valentino proposed to Betty at a *thé dansant* in aid of the Italian society for the prevention of cruelty to animals (an organisation that needed all the support it could get!). They were married in the Campidoglio, the Capitol of ancient Rome, on 28 October 1927.

They had four children, and on 8 September 1943, the day this story starts, Enrico was fifteen years old, Alec thirteen, Billy just eight and Teresa five.

Valentino, who had managed to avoid being sent to fight against his wife's fellow countrymen while Italy was still in the war on the side of Germany, was serving on the staff of a general in Turin. Betty and her children were at Casa San Marzano, the house at Colle Attivoli, overlooking Spoleto, which Valentino had bought in 1937 when he was second-in-command of a training school for officer cadets in that Umbrian town.

PART I
Friends and Enemies

On that memorable day, 8 September 1943, Betty was sketching from the terrace of Casa San Marzano. She never tired of the view over the valley, the woods and the distant mountains. The September afternoon sun was pleasantly warm but not hot and, apart from the clatter which her boisterous maid Serafina was making over the washing-up from lunch, all was tranquil.

Then she heard the front-door bell ring and Serafina's wooden clogs clumping out of the kitchen. A moment later the maid appeared to announce that Colonello Boldoni and his wife had called to see the Contessa. Betty stopped drawing and told Serafina to set chairs for her visitors on the terrace.

Colonello Boldoni, a squat man with bushy eyebrows and hair cut very short, had been on the staff of the Spoleto Military School at which Valentino had been second-in-command. Pompous, self-important and a great admirer of the Duce, he nevertheless made a point of keeping on good terms with Colonello di San Marzano. For the sake of solidarity with senior officers, Colonello Boldoni was generously prepared to overlook Valentino's inexplicable lapse in marrying an Englishwoman. She was very pretty and charming too, he had to admit, with her neat figure, curly chestnut hair and hazel eyes.

Upstairs in the children's room Betty's two older boys, Enrico and Alec, with their friend Marcello Cimicchi, were listening to the radio which, quietly tuned to the B.B.C. wavelength, was inaudible through the shutters to anyone outside. At a table Billy was teaching Teresa to play Beggar-my-Neighbour.

Suddenly the window was thrown open with a clatter and several excited faces appeared. 'The Armistice! The Armistice!'

Colonello Boldoni, who had been smiling politely before this interruption, glaced upwards, the smile frozen on his face. When the significance of what the children were shouting finally dawned on him, he performed a double-take worthy of Groucho Marx. Leaping to his feet, scarlet in the face with fury, he dashed his smart hat to the ground and stamped on it. Then, cursing, he rushed out of the gate and away towards the town, leaving his battered cap where it lay.

'Oh dear, I really must apologise.' An embarrassed Signora Boldoni reached down to retrieve her husband's headgear, but no one even heard her and she was nearly bowled over by a cascade of children erupting on to the terrace. Muttering more apologies, then realising that everyone was now oblivious of her presence, she followed in the wake of the irate Colonel, while in the first moments of jubilation Betty and the children rushed about shouting with joy, embracing each other and letting the unheeded voice of the English announcer blaze on into the still air.

When at last they paused for breath, Betty gasped, 'I must telephone Daddy.'

The line was engaged. She waited five minutes, then tried again, but still with no success. Meanwhile, the children were getting impatient.

'What shall we do, Mum?' Enrico asked. 'We can't just stay here.'

'We could go and see how the Germans are taking it.'

'Oh yes, do let's.' They charged off down the rough track that led to the main road, their mother hard put to it to keep up with them.

A procession of German vehicles was moving north, column upon column of buff-coloured traffic crawling ceaselessly along the road.

Enrico whispered to Betty, 'Do you think they're evacuating Italy?'

'I hope to God they are.'

She was curious to see what these 'glorious, invincible heroes' of Nazism looked like in the flesh. Some of the trucks had stopped for a rest under the trees and they watched the men moving about like any other human beings, goodlooking fair youths in their khaki, straight from North Africa, eating sauerkraut and black bread, washing, shaving, laughing quietly among themselves but indifferent to the passers-by.

London had announced the Armistice two hours before Rome. When the great news was eventually released, Italy gave one enormous whoop of joy. For several days euphoria reigned. Rumours multiplied: the Allies had made several landings, including one at Civitavecchia, it was reliably reported, and the Germans were getting out of Italy as fast as their flat, goose-stepping feet could carry them so as not to be cut off by the invading Allies, or by the gallant Italian forces which had now changed sides.

A few days later Betty was preparing lunch when her second son, Alec, who had been watching the main road from a hillock near the house, came running into the kitchen looking alarmed. 'The German traffic has switched direction. It's going south now.'

Betty took the pasta off the stove and ran to their vantage point overlooking the main road. Alec was right. The stream of buff-coloured vehicles was pouring south. She swore, ran back to the house for her telescope and returned with it to the hillock. Through the telescope the trucks looked new, and they were bristling with weapons of fresh and unknown shapes. The faces were fiercer, troops from the Fatherland or from northern Italian garrisons being rushed south to the front.

The full meaning of the situation quickly dispelled the euphoria of the past few days. Italy faced a German occupation. After their landings at Salerno, the Allies were pushing up the Peninsula, and at the time of the Armistice were in Calabria, while the Germans were now pouring in reinforcements over the Brenner Pass, making of Italy a vast camp, an arsenal, to stem the Allied advance.

Ever since the war had been declared Betty had listened in secret to the B.B.C., which had constantly broadcast reports of the repression and atrocities suffered by the people of occupied France and other countries at the hands of the Germans. Now, she knew, they would face the same terror methods – arrests, torture, deportations and the shooting of hostages.

In central Italy the people are an ancient race of dreamers, pacific and tolerant, little changed by the comings and goings of invaders through the centuries. Because of this the Germans took over bloodlessly and the population seemed to look on with indifference.

It was stiflingly hot and the drought had burned the countryside to ochre. The oppressive heat seemed to contain some threat. Day after day the Allied bombers passed over and they heard the bombing of Terni, some miles across the mountains, until much of the town was reduced to ruins. On hearing the planes, the boys would take the telescope and, hiding on the hillside, watch the lovely shining machines throbbing effortlessly through the cloudless sky. They knew that these were friends, despite the bombs and destruction that could rain down. Through the telescope the distinguishing marks seemed near enough to touch and they were thrilled by the proximity of their fellow countrymen.

Soon streams of refugees from the south invaded the countryside, camping in caves or huts in the mountains. Homeless and destitute, these poor people could expect no help from the Government, but had to depend on the kindness of others or on charitable or religious institutions. Often the roads and railways were the targets for the bombers, and always the air was full of noise, the drone of planes, bombs exploding or the rumble of distant guns.

About this time the fascists, who had lain low after the fall of Mussolini, perked up and became cock-a-hoop, keen to show their comrades-in-arms how zealous and efficient they were at harassing their own people.

One morning Betty and the children were finishing breakfast when they heard loud knocks on the front door. Serafina went to answer it and Betty, peering out of the window, saw two figures in uniform outside. Pushing Enrico and Alec quickly out of the back door, she told them to go through the vineyard into the wood and hide there until the coast was clear. Meanwhile, Serafina had shown the two men into the drawing room, where Betty went to see what they wanted. They were dressed in the uniform of the Fascist Militia and both were scowling.

'You are Signora di San Marzano?' the taller man asked.

'Yes. What can I do for you gentlemen?'

'We have come to search the house.'

'Really? And why, may I ask?'

'That is no concern of yours.'

'Oh, but it is. It happens to be my house, or rather my husband's – Colonello di San Marzano – perhaps you know him?'

'We have reason to believe that you have been listening to enemy broadcasts.'

'But Italy is no longer at war,' Betty protested. 'As neutrals we are surely entitled to listen to any broadcasts we please.'

'True patriots do not recognise the cowardly armistice concluded by the traitor Badoglio. We fight on at the side of our brave German allies.'

'I see. May I see your search warrant?'

'That will not be necessary.'

'Why? Does the law no longer apply now that our German allies have taken over?'

The smaller of the two fascists spoke for the first time. 'I should advise you not to be impudent, Signora. A list of suspected persons has been drawn up to prevent sabotage, hostile activities and rumour-mongering. Your name is on that list.'

'Why? Just because I am English?'

'You are an enemy alien and as such automatically under surveillance.'

'Even though my husband is a colonel in the Italian Army?'

'He is not here to exercise control over you.'

Betty flushed with anger. 'I find that remark insulting.'

Ignoring her, the two fascists moved over to the desk, pulling open the drawers and scanning the papers inside them. They made some show of reading Betty's letters, but as most of these were in English she doubted whether they gleaned much from them.

After they had glanced at the other downstairs rooms they proceeded upstairs, where in the children's playroom they found the wireless which had proclaimed the glad news of the Armistice.

'This we shall have to confiscate,' the shorter fascist announced.

Betty made them give her a receipt, but although she pretended to be indignant she was not greatly upset because she had concealed another and better radio in the bottom of an old oak chest, covered with tennis rackets and other sports gear. An old revolver belonging to Valentino, with its ammunition, was also hidden there, and Betty was relieved when the militiamen peered into it and passed on.

Looking pleased with themselves, the fascists gave her a curt nod and departed. She sent Billy to find her two older sons and tell them they could return.

Next morning the Bank Manager telephoned, asking Betty to call when she was in Spoleto. Sensing trouble, she went straight down to the Bank and was ushered into the Manager's office.

'I must apologise for bothering you, Contessa, but I thought you should know that your account is overdrawn.'

On inspecting the ledger, Betty found that the monthly allowance that Valentino made her had not been paid in since June. She pointed this out to the Manager, who looked embarrassed.

'I am infinitely sorry, Contessa, but what are we to do? Everything is in confusion. One can get no sense out of anyone.'

'You'll have to make me a loan until I can contact the Colonello.'

'Nothing would give me greater pleasure, Contessa, but most unfortunately Head Office has given instructions that no loans are to be given until further notice.' The Manager sighed deeply. 'For a banker to be forbidden to lend money is absurd. It is like a baker being forbidden to sell bread. But if I point that out to them I shall be sacked, and probably arrested as well.'

In the end Betty persuaded him to allow her a slightly larger overdraft, but the Manager made it clear that he was too frightened of being denounced by his own staff to grant her any further favours.

When she got home Betty tried to telephone Valentino, but she was told that the line would not be clear for some hours. She tried again several times that evening, but the number was always engaged. When she finally got through, it was only to be informed that the Colonello had been posted to a new station, the location of which could not be disclosed for security reasons.

The small monthly allowance that Betty had hitherto received from Valentino, the equivalent of little more than £12 sterling, was in any case too small to support a family of five. For the last two years, therefore, she had supplemented this by giving English lessons, selling her paintings and doing various odd jobs, so that there had always been enough, though only just enough, to live on.

The new station to which Valentino had been posted in August 1943 was Turin. For weeks he had been trying unsuccessfully to make contact with Betty, and when the news of the Armistice broke he was too worried about his family to join in the boisterous celebrations that were being held everywhere in the town. Instead, he rushed to the telephone, but so did about half the population – the half that was not drinking the health of Badoglio and death to the Germans and fascists – and the lines to Spoleto seemed to be permanently engaged.

Valentino would have been even more worried had he known that, owing to some bureaucratic bungle, the standing order whereby he made over part of his pay to his wife had ceased to function and that she had no means of support.

On 11 September Mario Bistrelli, his Staff Major, came into his office with a long face and put down a document on his desk.

'This has just come in.'

'This' was an order signed by General Gerstenheimer, the German Commander of the Turin Military Area, brief and to the point: 'All Italian officers of the rank of major and above will report to G.H.Q., Turin, at 1400 hours on 12 September 1943.'

'You know Gerstenheimer's Aide de Camp, don't you, Mario?'

Bistrelli nodded. 'Slightly, yes.'

'Go and see if you can find him and ask him what it's all about.'

When Bistrelli had gone, Valentino again tried unsuccessfully to telephone Betty. Within less than an hour the Staff Major returned. 'He was cagey at first, but I inveighed against Badoglio and the Armistice and in the end he came clean. We are all to be sent to Germany to continue the war at the side of our dear German allies!'

'I might have guessed.'

'What shall we do?'

'I know what I intend to do: follow the excellent example of three-quarters of the troops under our command and push off into the countryside.'

'May I come with you?'

'Of course, if you really want to. You know the risks as well as I do.'

They packed their civilian clothes and personal possessions into suitcases, loaded them into a staff car whose tank they filled with army petrol, and drove out of the barracks, taking the road leading to Aosta. When they reached the foothills of the Alps they pulled off the main road, drove a few kilometres up a hilly by-road, and stopped to change into civilian clothes. They left their uniforms in the car, which they then abandoned, and started to walk into the mountains. Three days later they joined up with a band of partisans.

Meanwhile, in Umbria, the atmosphere had become very tense. No one knew what would happen or who would be pounced on next. Rumours circulated, people disappeared. Women seemed vague as to the whereabouts of husbands and sons, and everyone was careful never to ask questions about male relatives.

Rampoldi, the artist, came to warn Betty that the fascists were rounding people up. He advised them to hide.

'Anyway, one of you should always be on guard at the top of that track overlooking the road where everyone must pass to come up to this house. Take good heed of what I say, because I know a thing or two. But don't search me out or telephone me. I'm disappearing.'

So the older boys took it in turns and spent long, weary hours squatting in the gorse keeping a look-out. Nothing happened, but Betty received the same warning from her close friend Angelina de Marchis and several others, until she felt she could no longer ignore it.

She did not know where to go, what to do or to whom to turn for advice. She could trust no one absolutely, and if they decided to go into hiding it was essential that their flight should be kept secret.

She was sitting outside the door, calling to mind all their friends who might have been able to help had they not been in the same plight themselves. Then she had an idea. Against the far wall of the courtyard stood the house of the *contadini* (peasants) – three rooms over stables and pigsties. It housed nine people, but they seemed to fit in comfortably, perhaps because they were all, except one, diminutive. The exception was the mother of the family, Giulia, a big jovial woman with a pleasant face and unfailing smile. Pierino, her husband, stood only about four foot high, but he was a most genial little man, besotted about his five little daughters.

With them lived the old grandparents, miniature people like Pierino, who toiled in the fields from dawn to dusk. They, too, doted on their grandchildren, but the little girls were not spoiled by all this adoration, being helpful, polite and good-natured. Altogether, it was an ideal family to have at such close quarters. In fact, they all lived as intimate friends, with the give and take of good neighbours. Now, in her perplexity, Betty realised that Giulia was perhaps the one person to whom she could turn. She went to see her.

Giulia thought for several moments. 'Why, yes, I think I might be able to find you a safe hiding place, Signora.'

She was a real benefactor, Betty felt, as she looked affectionately at

Giulia's plump, kindly face. Her instinct had not been wrong. She decided to confide everything.

'Look, Giulia, I want to explain our situation quite candidly. I have no money whatsoever. The small monthly sum my husband used to send me has ceased. I don't know where he is and I can't get in touch with him. My savings are finished, and with the German occupation I can't give English lessons any more. I'm facing complete destitution. I'm desperate for any sort of refuge, but I can only offer a nominal rent.'

'I'm sure my sister at Roselli will help you. If you can pay her something, well and good. If you can't –' Giulia shrugged, as if to say it wouldn't matter.

'We don't know what will happen to us, of course,' Betty pointed out. 'We may all be deported to Germany, put in prison or killed, so if your sister helps us, it will be out of Christian charity. I have heard the fascists are after us, so we must get away as quickly and secretly as possible.'

By this time the kind-hearted Giulia was in tears. She said she would telephone to the post office at Roselli and have her sister called to the phone. After a long wait, a strange conversation couched in double meanings elicited the information that Piera had a loft, a most unsuitable place but still a refuge from the elements and the wrath of man, and that they could have it if they really needed it.

Pierino offered to walk the twenty odd miles to Roselli to arrange things for them. He also had a cart, which he said could be harnessed to Tessa's old donkey, Caterina, to take their baggage. Betty thanked them both profusely.

When she got back to her own home, she took the two older boys aside and told them her plan.

'Didn't Dad once get a job for one of Piera's relations?' Enrico asked.

Betty had forgotten about this, but now she remembered. 'Oh yes, he was out of work and Daddy found him a job as guardian of the woods. You're quite right, Enrico. It might help, I suppose.'

They were still discussing the flight to Roselli when there was a tap on the front door. Outside Betty found old Clementina, the grandmother from the peasants' house.

She bobbed a curtsey, her wrinkled little eyes full of mysterious twinklings. 'May I speak to you, Signora Contessa?'

Betty took her into the dining room, and as she shut the door the old woman drew something out from beneath her apron. It was a savings book which she thrust into Betty's hand. She was trembling.

'Oh, Signora, please take this, it's all my savings but I know you're in need and I would like you to have it and I'm sorry it's not more. Oh dear me, don't tell my family I'm giving it to you, not that they wouldn't want me to, and oh how dreadful for you this terrible war is and that rascal Mussolini, may his soul be damned! It won't buy much, not with the prices they ask these days, but I want you to have it, for what it's worth, which is little enough, as I say.'

She ended up quite breathless and, having given vent to her feelings, flopped on an upright chair, her face in her hands.

Betty was so overcome by this unforeseen generosity that she could do nothing but press the book into the old woman's hand and embrace her. She thought of those savings being put away month by month against old age, yet now Clementina was offering them all to her, a foreigner.

Betty could only persuade her to keep the money by assuring her that she had enough for the moment. Indeed, she did have a precious five pound note from her last trip to England, which she had decided to sell to Alfonso de Marchis, who had always been so good to them. She knew he would give her the current exchange rate for the Allied-Occupied Zone, 400 lire to the pound, so she would be able to give Piera something for the room, and perhaps with the rest she could buy vegetables and eggs to supplement her store of flour and olive oil.

But Clementina's gesture helped to restore their faith in humanity and to dispel their low spirits.

That evening, after the two younger children had gone to bed, Betty impressed upon Enrico and Alec how vitally important it was to keep their flight to Roselli secret.

'You musn't say a word to anyone, not even Billy and Teresa. Pierino is going over there tomorrow to make sure we are expected and to see everything is all right.'

'Can I go with him?' Alec asked.

Enrico frowned. 'Why not me?'

Betty reflected that she could do with an independent account of the Bussoni *ménage*. Although two years the younger, Alec was more observant than Enrico. He would be sure to note their various reactions to the prospect of housing a refugee family in their loft. On the other hand, she must be careful not to offend her eldest son.

'I think it's a good idea for one of you to go and spy out the land, but I don't think I can really spare you, Enrico. There are a hundred and one things to do here. So I'd like you to go, Alec, provided Pierino doesn't mind. You'd better go and ask him.'

Pierino was pleased to let Alec accompany him, and they set off together next morning, while Betty and Enrico took it in turns to keep look-out.

Enrico was on guard after lunch when he spotted three uniformed figures coming up the track that led past the house. He rushed back to raise the alarm. Betty told him to slip out at the back and hide in the woods.

Enrico looked worried. 'I'd rather stay here with you.'

'You're the one in danger, darling. I'm told they're even press-ganging teenagers into their wretched militia these days. We don't want them to grab you or ship you off to Germany, do we?'

In fact, after all the warnings she had received, Betty was sure the fascists were coming to arrest the whole family.

'Billy! Teresa!' she called. 'Come here at once!'

But her two younger children had disappeared somewhere and she herself could not escape without them. She ran upstairs and fetched the revolver from the bottom of the oak chest.

'Most fascists are bullies,' she said to herself, 'and bullies are generally cowards. Besides, they won't expect a woman to pull a gun on them. I should be able to lock them in the cellar while we escape.'

Then she remembered that Alec would be returning here and might run straight into their arms. She was a hostage.

She pushed the revolver back under the sports gear in the chest, then went to a bedroom window from which she could watch the track. A few minutes later the three fascists appeared.

The leader, a moronic-looking fellow with a receding chin, sported a pistol in his belt holster, a black shirt, breeches and a little black fez. Behind him slouched a heavy, ape-like figure. He wore jackboots, his hands were sunk deep in his pockets, he was unshaven and frowning. The third man seemed apprehensive and kept peering nervously about him.

Betty decided that they looked more ludicrous than menacing, but she had no doubt that they could behave viciously if given the chance.

Just as they came level with the open gate, Serafina, who had not heard the alarm, appeared from an outhouse. She saw them, gave a frightened squeak and fled towards the house. The third fascist stopped dead and glared after her. The other two took no notice and passed on and eventually their nervous comrade followed them. Evidently, they were bent on some other mischief. Betty heaved a sigh of relief and went to find Enrico.

After Mussolini's rescue from his prison on the Gran Sasso by the German paratroops led by Otto Skorzeny, the Duce had been encouraged by the Führer to re-form his scattered and demoralised supporters into a new Fascist Republican Militia. Despite German pressure, however, the flow of volunteers had been decidedly sluggish, and fascist officials were accustomed to finding that almost every home they visited was inhabited entirely by women and children. It was then that they had started to enlist teenagers, some of them attracted by the uniforms, whips and guns.

Since the Armistice most fascists had been anxious to get out of uniform, dissociate themselves from the past and put themselves 'on the right side'. Those who still openly avowed their creed either still hoped for a German victory, despite all the pointers in the opposite direction, or were unhappily aware that they were too deeply compromised, had nothing to lose and might as well go on enjoying the fruits of power as long as they could.

Alec returned from Roselli just after dark, looking tired and complaining of a thirst like the Sahara Desert.

'Where's Pierino?' Betty asked.

'He had to take a package to someone in Spoleto, so I came on home by myself.'

Telling Serafina to look after the two younger children, Betty took Alec and Enrico into the living room and poured Alec a large glass of home-made lemonade.

'Well, how did it go?'

'They've offered us the loft, at least Pierino says they have, but they gabbled and argued so much between themselves it was jolly difficult to make out what they were getting at.'

Betty pointed out that arrangements like this always required a great deal of talk.

'Remember, we're asking them to take a big risk by sheltering us,' Enrico added.

Alec drained his glass of lemonade and poured himself some more. 'The man – Piera's husband, that is – didn't say much. He's called Domenico, by the way. I don't think Piera herself is too keen on having us.'

'That's odd. She was the one Giulia spoke to on the telephone – she's her sister, you know. She could have turned us down then.'

'I may be wrong, of course, but that's what I felt. She kept going on about all the other families who had more room and could give us better quarters.'

Betty sighed. 'Oh dear.'

'Actually, it was the old *nonna* who eventually weighed in on our side. After they had been yattering on for hours, she told them all to shut up. Then she took me outside and led me up the steps to the loft. "Will that do?" she asked. I thanked her and said of course it would. "Then you shall have it," she said.'

Betty laughed. 'Good old *nonna*! The grannies are generally the ones who take the vital decisions, especially among the *contadini*.'

'All the same,' Alec said with a frown, 'I don't think the rest of the family are all that pleased about our coming. Piera kept on saying that the loft was no sort of place for a lady. I tried to tell her you weren't at all stuck up' – 'Thank you, darling,' Betty murmured – 'but she said you would be disgusted when you saw the hovel they were offering.'

'Beggars can't be choosers, can they?'
'She says there are rats in the loft. Teresa won't like that.'
'Neither shall I. I'll take some rat poison – soon get rid of them. Meanwhile don't say anything to Teresa.'

Apart from the peasant family next door, the only people who knew they were going were Alfonso and Angelina de Marchis. Betty decided to run across the fields and say goodbye to them.
'We're off!'
Alfonso nodded approvingly. 'You are wise, Betty. We shall miss you abominably, but it's getting more dangerous here every day.'
'I know you won't breathe a word to a soul,' Betty said, 'but if Valentino turns up you can tell him why we decided to go.'
'Of course,' Angelina promised, 'and we'll try to keep you posted with news.'
Alfonso not only bought Betty's five pound note but also insisted on lending her some money, although she knew that he himself was in difficulties. She ran back through the fields feeling immensely rich, but very sad at parting with her closest friends. Who could say when, if ever, she would see them again?

The fall of Mussolini and the Armistice with the Allies had come as bitter blows to Cesarino Matafia, *Podesta* (Mayor) of Spoleto. To add insult to injury he had been sent for by the German Major commanding the Spoleto garrison and upbraided as if he were personally responsible for these disasters. Since the Armistice the Italian troops under the German Major's command had been melting away like snow in spring, and the *Podesta* was left in no doubt about what would happen to him if he deserted his post or tried to change sides, like the treacherous Badoglio.
'Herr Major, I beseech you not to suggest such a wicked thing,' he protested. 'Have I not been the Duce's loyal servant ever since his great March on Rome? Did I not collect over a thousand wedding rings from the married women of this city to help support his civilising mission against the barbarian Haile Selassie in Ethiopia? Am I not the senior *podesta* in Umbria? Did I not –?'
'Perhaps,' the German Major interrupted crossly. 'It's the same story from all you Italians. Yet every single Italian officer in my command has vanished, and no doubt a lot of them will defect to the enemy if we give them half a chance. Shoot first and ask questions later, that's what we shall do when we catch up with them.'

The *Podesta* turned pale. Then a bright thought struck him. 'Herr Major, you know about that Englishwoman at Colle Attivoli?'

'No, what about her?'

'The wife of Colonello di San Marzano. He's one of our decadent aristocrats. Calls himself "Conte" di San Marzano. I heard from Colonello Boldoni that she was listening to foreign broadcasts. I sent two of our militiamen to search her house and they confiscated her wireless. A long time before that I had had her placed under surveillance.'

'So I should hope. If she's English she should have been interned.'

'Precisely what I recommended, Herr Major, but they wouldn't listen to me.'

'Well, you take your instructions from me now. You'd better see she's put out of harm's way.'

The *Podesta* beamed. 'Most certainly, Herr Major. You can rely on me implicitly.'

He returned frowning to his office in the Town Hall. At the small table next to Matafia's large desk Sergio Gragnelli, his young clerk, was preparing papers for him to sign.

The *Podesta* was mumbling to himself, complaining about the cavalier treatment he had received at the hands of the German Major. Then Sergio heard him murmur: 'One job I do look forward to is stringing up that Marzano woman and her brats from five lamp-posts before the English arrive.'

The clerk placed the documents on the *Podesta*'s desk and slipped out of the office.

Within an hour of Matafia's mumbled threat Serafina was roused from her afternoon siesta by loud knocking at the front door. Opening it, she was surprised to find Ottavio Gragnelli, the portly and ponderous baker from whom Betty always bought her bread. He was red-faced, panting and perspiring. His bicycle was propped against the garden gate and it was clear that he must have pedalled it most of the way up the steep hill from his shop in Spoleto to Colle Attivoli.

'Ottavio! Whatever is the matter?'

'I must speak to the Contessa at once.'

'But she's resting.'

'Then go and rouse her.'

'But Ottavio, what has happened?'

The baker stamped his foot in exasperation, took a handkerchief from his pocket and mopped his brow.

'Stop asking stupid questions, woman, and do as I say. It's a matter of life and death.'

'*Mamma mia*!' Serafina turned and ran into the house.

Betty, who was not resting but sketching from her bedroom window, appeared a minute later, invited Signor Gragnelli into the drawing room and offered him wine.

'No thank you, Contessa, just a glass of water in a moment, if you please. But there's no time to lose. I have some grave news for you.'

Betty waved him to an armchair and sat down herself.

'Well, Ottavio, let's hear the worst.'

'You know that my nephew Sergio works in the office of the *Podesta*.' Betty nodded. 'Well, an hour ago he came running round to my shop in a great state.'

'Matafia is going to have us arrested, I suppose.'

'Worse than that, I'm afraid. Sergio says he intends to have you all killed.'

'Killed?'

'Yes Contessa. You and your four children. Hanged from lamp-posts, the barbarian.'

'Isn't he afraid of what will happen to him when the Allies get here?'

'He'll run away, I expect. Sergio thinks the Germans put him up to this, but he's committed plenty of ugly deeds without their prompting. Villain!'

'I'm very grateful to you for warning me, Ottavio.'

'You must flee, Contessa. Where will you go?'

Betty replied cautiously. 'I'm not sure. Anyway it may be better for you not to know in case they question you. If anyone asks what you were doing here, tell him I left my bread in your shop this morning by mistake.'

'Very well, Contessa. You are so calm. I admire you.'

Betty smiled, but she did not feel very calm.

'I'll get you that glass of water. Then we'll make sure the coast is clear before you start back.'

When she had seen the baker safely off the premises, she found her eldest son and took him aside. Without letting him know of the *Podesta*'s threat to have them all hanged, she told him they were now in great danger and would have to flee to Roselli as soon as they could gather their things together.

'Tonight?'

'No, we might look suspicious and get stopped at night.'

'Early tomorrow morning, then?'

'That's right.'

'I'll go and warn the others, shall I?'

'Wait a minute, Enrico.' Betty laid a hand on his arm. 'Listen, I don't want them to be frightened. We shall have to turn it all into a game. The winter's coming and there are sure to be times when we find ourselves cold, wet and hungry. But whatever happens, you and I must make sure it's all part of a big adventure, exciting but never really dangerous. Do you see what I mean?'

Enrico looked pleased. At fifteen it is satisfying to be treated as an adult. 'You can count on me, Mummy.' A thought struck him. 'What are you going to do about your valuables, jewellery and such like?'

'I don't know. We'll have to hide them, I suppose.'

'Why don't we dig a hole in the garden and bury them all? We could pretend it was buried treasure. You know how much Alec and Billy love *Treasure Island*.'

Betty smiled. 'What a good idea, Enrico!'

'Billy and Teresa wouldn't be much good at digging, so they could take over as look-outs to warn us if the fascists are coming.'

'Splendid. You would make an excellent Chief of Staff.'

'Like Daddy?'

'That's right.'

'Where is he now, do you think?'

'I wish I knew. But he told me once that when the Allies got nearer he would try to desert to the partisans. I've heard nothing from him since the Armistice, so he may already have done so.'

'How will he know where we've gone? If he gets back here, I mean.'

'Giulia will tell him. Now, go and find the others and tell them about burying our treasure. Post Billy and Teresa as look-outs and make it sound important, Enrico. Then you and Alec fetch spades and a pick from the toolshed and start digging your hole.'

Betty went upstairs to the nursery and emptied the big wooden box containing the children's toys. In the bottom she packed some of her favourite pictures, wrapped in linen, and on top of them her jewel box, the silver and the best pieces of china. She found a smaller box in which she placed some of the children's best loved books and toys to take with them if there was room. She then packed the family's winter clothes and personal possessions into suitcases, leaving only their night things.

'Poor Caterina, I hope she can pull all this as far as Roselli,' Betty thought, surveying their baggage. By the time she got downstairs again, Enrico and Alec had already dug a sizeable trench at the bottom of the small vineyard adjoining the garden.

'Phew! This is hard work, Mum.' Alec threw out two large flints from the bottom of the pit. 'I'm getting down to rock.'

'I'll take a turn.'

Betty climbed into the trench and relieved Alec of his spade. In another half-hour she and Enrico had made a hole big enough for the wooden box.

Billy and Teresa were relieved from their look-out posts so that they could join in the game of burying the treasure. Serafina too came out to admire the good work, and with the aid of a strap Enrico and Betty lowered the box into the pit. The boys quickly heaped back the soil, trod it down and covered the patch with brushwood.

'What are we going to do with the revolver, Mum?' Enrico was scraping soil off his clogs. 'Take it with us?'

'Better not. There's been an order for all firearms to be handed in on pain of death. If they searched the cart and found it, we'd be for the high jump.'

'We should have buried it along with the "treasure",' Alec said.

Enrico shook his head. 'No, someone might have heard us digging and reported us. If the revolver was found with the other stuff, they'd know it was ours.'

'What about the roof?' Alec suggested. 'You put the daggers up there, didn't you, Mummy?'

'It would still be our property,' Enrico pointed out, 'and we should be answerable for it.'

'That clump of bushes down the track. We could bury it under them and we'd know where to find it when we come back, too.'

'That's a very good idea, Alec,' Betty said.

After Enrico had oiled the revolver and wrapped it in rags, they put it in an old cake tin. The tin sported a seventeenth-century maiden mincing incongruously across the lid. Betty carried it cautiously down the track to the bushes. Every time they started digging, however, they heard footsteps approaching and had to stop and pretend to be digging up plants or looking at the landscape. At last the deed was done, and a great weight lifted from their minds.

When they returned to the house Serafina drew Betty aside and told her she had decided to stay at Colle Attivoli rather then go with them to Roselli.

'You must do whatever you think best, but we shall miss you.'

As she said this Betty realised, rather to her surprise, that she was speaking no more than the truth. They were often exasperated by the great buxom wench, bursting with health, noisy and vulgar, as she clattered round the house on wooden clogs, her harsh voice maltreating opera as she maltreated their dishes. All her clothes were too tight and too short, and patches of bare Serafina could be seen in unexpected places. But she had a good heart and was utterly loyal.

Betty knew what lay behind her decision. She was having an affair with the electrician and preferred to face the fascists rather than risk losing this chance of matrimony. Her greatest wish was to have a man of her own and get married. Her many casual relationships did not satisfy her and she felt she was getting on in years. For peasants, to have arrived at the late twenties unmarried signified being on the shelf.

'I expect you can move in with Giulia and Pierino,' Betty told her. 'I'll give you a key and you can keep an eye on this house.'

'What shall I do if the Germans or the fascists come for you?'

'Tell them I have taken my children to Rome.'
'Very well, Signora.'

During the afternoon Betty told the three younger children about the great adventure they were all going to embark on next morning.

'We are going to live right in the country for a while, a long way from Spoleto. Tomorrow, if you like, we can pretend to be gipsies.'

'We shall look like gipsies, shan't we,' Billy said, 'with skinny old Caterina pulling that broken-down cart.'

Teresa protested. 'Don't be so rude. Caterina is a lovely donkey, not a bit gipsyish.'

Betty warned them that life in the country would be very different to what they were used to. 'We shall all have to learn lots of new and interesting things.'

Alec asked: 'What sort of things, Mummy?'

'Well, Daddy hasn't been able to send me any money for some time, so we shan't be able to buy much, and any food we can find for ourselves will be welcome. We can look for chestnuts and mushrooms, but we must be careful about *funghi* because some are poisonous.'

Teresa said she knew where there were lots of blackberries. Alec asked if he should take his catapult. 'I might bag a rabbit.'

'Or a wild boar,' Billy added.

'We can collect firewood and learn to cook over an open fire.'

Billy was all for this. 'Like Red Indians,' he said. 'What fun!'

'It may not be fun all the time,' Betty pointed out. 'We may sometimes be uncomfortable and cold. Tomorrow, for instance, I expect we shall all be tired by the time we get to Roselli.'

'I bet old Caterina will be,' Billy said.

'We're sure to have our problems, but I hope there'll be many compensations.'

'What are compenstations?' Teresa asked. 'Those places where Billy's trains stop?'

They all laughed. Betty tried to explain. 'Compensations are good things that make up for bad ones.'

'Like partisans making up for Germans and fascists,' Alec said.

'Or better still blowing them up.' Billy let out a big boom.

Betty stood up. 'Well, we must all have an early night. We shall have to be up before light and away at dawn. You'd better all have a bath too. You may not get another for a long time.'

Billy and Teresa went off to prepare an extra large feed for Caterina, while Enrico checked and cleaned the harness for the cart. Alec went on look-out, and Betty herself prepared knapsacks of food for the next day.

After Billy and Teresa had been sent to bed, Betty and the two elder boys loaded the cart by lantern light, rejecting this and that until they were down to essentials – two suitcases, a blanket each, two padded quilts, a bag of flour, a sack of macaroni, a jar of oil and a few, alas very few, odds and ends of food – no luxuries or frills of any sort.

Enrico and Alec offered to stay on look-out by turns through the night, but Betty sent them to get what sleep they could. She knew that fear was a bad bed-fellow and that she herself could not rest that night, so she drew up a chair to her bedroom window from which she could watch the courtyard.

Every moment she expected to hear footsteps, followed by a banging on the door proclaiming that the fascists had arrived to take them away. She planned that if this happened they would all slip out at the back and make for the woods.

But the night wore on, without incident, and Betty dozed a little in her chair.

PART II
Refugees and Prisoners

Serafina's clattering clogs jerked Betty fully awake. It was still dark, but she could hear the patter of rain on the roof.

The maid drew back the curtains. '*Che brutto tempo*! You cannot set forth in this.'

In Italy everything comes to a halt when it rains, the general concensus being that to get wet will surely lead to pneumonia and a quick death.

'I prefer a drop of rain to Matafia's thugs,' Betty said, reflecting with satisfaction that the fascists were most unlikely to set off for Colle Attivoli until it stopped raining. 'Will you wake the children, please, Serafina?'

Under Betty's supervision the boys harnessed Caterina to the cart, a regular pedlar's outfit, with a saucepan hanging underneath, and a lantern, rope, axe and other odds and ends tied to the bars.

Their baggage, piled high, was capped by a little pair of clogs, all that could be seen of Teresa, sunk among the packages.

Serafina and everyone from the peasants' house came out to wish them God-speed, and the faithful Giulia walked with them to the top of the next hill. They left her there, standing like a statue, tears and rain streaming down her face, until a bend in the road hid her from view.

'Now we really are refugees,' Betty thought. She never expected to see their home again. The Germans would destroy it or the battle would sweep it away, as it had so many millions of homes. They were homeless outcasts, surrounded by enemies, with no one to turn to.

At least the tense hours of waiting were over. They were still together and free. Feeling well and strong, they sang as they trudged along behind the cart. They had thrown in their lot with the thousands of refugees and runaways hiding in the hills, many of them later to combine into the bands of partisans which were to be such a plague to the Germans.

Betty knew that walking any distance was going to be a problem, because the children had long grown out of their shoes, new ones were unobtainable and they were shod with wooden clogs.

By midday they were in open country, having put about twelve kilometres between themselves and Spoleto, but Alec and Billy were limping and looking tired. It was still drizzling and Betty asked Alec, who was at Caterina's head, to lead the donkey and cart into the shelter of a small wood that ran beside the road.

'Take your clogs and socks off, and I'll have a look at your feet before lunch.'

Having put plasters on their blisters, she arranged their frugal meal of dry bread and apples on a tree stump. The rain stopped and the children munched away happily.

After lunch they plodded on, and when her children fell silent and began to look tired again, Betty started a game of 'I Spy'. In mid-afternoon, however, the rain started to teem down in earnest and soon they were all drenched.

'There's jolly little I can spy except something beginning with R,' Billy said when his turn came round.

'Rain!' they shouted in unison.

Billy scowled. 'All right, you spy something, then.'

Roselli was a tiny village right up in the mountains, hidden from view by a fold in the hills until one came suddenly upon it, a little hamlet of a dozen hovels built of big square stones blackened with age, all the houses clinging together and presenting a solid, almost fortified front to the newcomer, like a castle in miniature.

The mountains were covered with chestnut woods and the sandy soil had formed into strange folds and creases, eroded by numerous tiny streams flowing down small canyons, with thick undergrowth along the banks which afforded excellent shelter for persons wishing to pass unseen from one point to another.

From a distance the village looked picturesque, but closer acquaintance brought disillusionment. The houses were jammed so close together that the unpaved alley which served as a street was a sea of mud in wet weather, and in the summer a breeding ground for bluebottles buzzing in the decaying rubbish thrown out by the villagers. For everything was flung out of the front doors and windows into the seething, stinking lane, and every few yards an outcrop of the rock on which the village was built projected through the mud to stub unwary toes.

The light was beginning to fade when they finally reached Roselli, soaked to the skin and exhausted, but curious to see their new home.

Piera's house was almost the poorest in the village, dark, gloomy and tumbledown, crushed in by its neighbours as if they were trying to squeeze all life out of the black stones.

Betty hammered on the door. Their luck was in, for it was opened by the old grandmother who had shown Alec the loft and promised they could have it.

'*Mamma mia, povera gente*!' She gazed aghast at the weary-looking woman on the threshold, the bedraggled children, the disconsolate donkey, water dripping from its coat, the laden cart. 'What terrible weather! Come in, come in.'

The front door opened on to a vast kitchen, the width of the house, lit only by one small window. The heavy beams of the ceiling pressed down to a few inches above head height, and only the table in the centre caught the light. All else was lost in gloom. Strange shapes and figures seemed to be all around, half seen in the murky atmosphere.

Many people were seated round the fire, a huge open hearth big enough for the children to sit in the chimney corners with their bare toes almost in the embers.

Piera Bussoni bustled up, clicking her tongue, as steam rose in clouds from their soaking garments.

'I'm sorry to inflict this lot of gipsies on you,' Betty said apologetically, 'but I couldn't find anywhere else to go.'

'What a disaster! But we have nowhere fit for you, Signora. We all sleep in one room as it is, you know.'

'Giulia said you had very kindly offered us your loft.'

'But it's not fit for you, Signora,' the woman repeated, shaking her head in anguish. 'It's dirty too. There are rats.'

'All we want is a roof over our heads,' Betty assured her.

They dragged in their luggage with the help of some youths, while Enrico saw to the donkey and cart. They were then shown their sleeping quarters, directly above and the same size as the kitchen and reached by a rickety wooden stair.

The window in the loft had been pushed into a hole in the wall, but not cemented in, and fresh air also came in abundantly through the gaps in the roof tiles. The floor was uneven brick and filthy, and there was no furniture. They spread the tarpaulin on the floor and on it any bedding that was not wet. Betty then went down to prepare their soup over the common fireplace.

They ate quickly, but before going to bed Betty drew Piera aside and murmured, 'Where's the –?'

The woman waved her hand vaguely at the dark night outside. 'Or, if you prefer it, there's the stable. We all go there when it is cold or raining.'

She put a lantern into Betty's hand and showed them to the stable, directly below the kitchen. They all trooped in, but staggered back as the stench hit them. Across one corner a huge gaunt pig was pegged in, glaring at them in the dim light with eyes made fierce by hunger, stamping in its own filth. Nearby was a poor cow, up to its hocks in muck, and all around had been thrown firewood, old tins and refuse of every sort.

Returning to the house, Betty protested to Piera: 'Look here, we can't use that stable. Haven't you got a *vaso da notte* of some sort for us?'

Piera shook her head. 'Perhaps tomorrow I can find someone in the village who could lend one, but tonight I can't help you. We have only one pot for the whole family.'

They had no lights, and they were so tired that they just lay down on their blankets without undressing. The children dropped off, but it was a long time before Betty slept. She could hear the rats scurrying about and watched the scudding clouds through the roof.

Later the peasant family went to bed, stumbling through into a tiny room off the loft, hardly big enough for two people but made to sleep seven. The children had to make do with sacks of straw on the floor, except for the little one, who lay squeezed between her parents in the bed.

There was no door to the room, so all undressing could be watched from Betty's corner of the loft. But for the peasants undressing was limited to removing one outer garment. Piera went to bed in her black petticoat, and Domenico in a pair of gloriously patched pants and shirt.

In the half light of a cold dawn Betty was roused by the peasant family trooping through the loft, picking their way round the prostrate forms stretched out on the floor, out through the door and down the wooden stair.

Billy sat up, scratching his thigh. 'I've been bitten, Mummy.'

'Probably fleas in the hay. With any luck we'll get immune in time.'

'What does "immune" mean?'

'You still get bitten, but you don't feel the bites any more.'

'Well, I hope I get immune jolly soon. I don't half itch.'

The other children were yawning and opening their eyes sleepily. 'We'd better go and see if there's any food going,' Betty said.

For breakfast that and every following day they stood in company with the peasants round the bare kitchen table on which Piera placed a huge bowl of something hot and steaming, smelling of herbs, and very welcome at that early hour.

Alec took a cautious spoonful. 'What is it?' he whispered to his mother.

'Dried broad beans, I think.'

The dried beans, often the consistency of shotgun pellets, were simmered for several hours in an earthenware jug in the embers. Then oil and herbs were added and the brew was poured boiling over slices of bread in a bowl rather like a wash-basin. There was enough to feed six families.

They stood round, dipping their spoons into the common mess, and all ate together, rapidly and silently, a solemn ritual.

After a few days Betty found that the hard beans gave her pains, so she switched to acorn coffee without sugar or milk. It was nasty, but she became accustomed to it. Though it did not alleviate hunger, it comforted the innards, and she preferred hunger to pains.

The Bussoni family numbered seven. The grandparents were both in their late seventies. The old man, lean, gnarled and bent, was called Sabatino. It was his wife Carrera, large and motherly, who had welcomed them on arrival.

Sabatino worked on the vegetable patch and gathered all the firewood for the house. Every day he plodded up to the woods with his chopper, and in the evening he would drag home heavy bundles of brushwood. Periodically he would borrow a donkey and make several journeys into the forest to bring down the logs which he had cut. These he sold, not by weight but by the square metre, and all judged by eye.

Sabatino's son Domenico, a taciturn, rather surly man of about forty, was not a peasant but worked, despite an injured leg, in the mines at Morgnano. Domenico's wife was Piera, the sister of Betty's dear neighbour Giulia at Colle Attivoli, but she had little of Giulia's warmth and kindness. Betty always had a feeling that Piera tolerated them merely in the hope that some time in the distant future they might be able to reward her. Certainly, she was not as frank and open as most of the local people, but stark poverty had probably made her hard and suspicious.

What Betty paid her out of their meagre store of money was quite sufficient for the loft and for their frugal breakfasts. But times were hard and Betty realised that the family might get into trouble with the authorities if their presence were discovered.

Domenico and Piera had a nine-year-old son, Antonio, and two little girls, Sabatina and Silvana. Antonio was only about four-foot high, cross-eyed and sallow. His large, slightly pointed ears gave him the appearance of a malevolent elf, though they were to discover that he was far from unintelligent and could be helpful if he felt so inclined.

The first job after breakfast was to seek permanent quarters for

Caterina. The previous night Enrico had found the little donkey a shed slightly more salubrious than Piera's stable, but she could not stay there.

Piera told them there was a farmer called Favi at Pian della Noce, a small hamlet about half a mile away across the fields, who might give her a home.

'He's pretty well off and he's got small children of his own.'

They found Favi tending his vines. He looked good-natured and took little persuading. Teresa kissed Caterina on the nose and choked back a tear when they said goodbye. Partly to take Teresa's mind off this sad farewell, Betty announced that she intended to rearrange the loft.

'Look, we are going to make it as much like a home as we can.'

She had started sweeping the floor, but the cracks between the uneven bricks were so wide that most of the dirt fell into them.

'Alec, go and find Piera and see if she can lend us something to put our clothes in,' Betty said.

'Have you got any string, Mum?' Enrico asked.

'Yes, I brought some. It's in that box, I think.'

'Well, if we stretch a piece across that corner and hang our tarpaulin over it, we can have our bathroom and lavatory behind it.'

'Good idea, Enrico.'

Alec returned with a deal case for their clothes. 'She's got an old table she says we can have too, but it's very heavy. Help me carry it up, will you, Enrico.'

Billy followed his older brothers out to see what he could scrounge around the place. He returned with a seatless chair which he had found in the stable. 'Look, Mum, we can fix the tin basin in here and turn it into a washstand.'

The basin fitted perfectly. 'Well done, Billy,' Betty said. The little boy beamed.

Enrico and Alec were staggering up the wooden stairs carrying the table. Behind them came a triumphant Piera, bearing a superb *vaso da notte* of heavy china with an intricate pattern of convolvulus all over it. Not a chip, not a mark, spoiled its pristine brightness, and it seemed altogether too glorious an object for its lowly function.

Piera showed them how to empty it. 'Just tip it out of the window, so –' she said, with an expansive gesture.

They looked out. Underneath them was the kitchen window and below that a large dung heap with all the refuse and manure from the stable, which had just been cleaned, steaming in the morning sun just below the kitchen.

As they arranged their things around the room it began to look quite homely. In a place where they were cut off from everything familiar except each other, their personal possessions, few though they were, took on a new significance; their clogs and hobnailed boots in a row in the corner, old coats on nails on the wall, their few books piled on the table and a small reproduction of the Sacred Heart, which Angelina de Marchis's daughter, little Magiu, had thrust into Betty's hand as she said goodbye, pinned above their bed.

Betty gazed out of the window. The view compensated for a great deal: lovely, gentle Umbria, fold upon fold of wooded hills, and in the blue distance Perugia, with little villages in the far plain like the background of a Raphael picture.

She was roused from her reverie by high-pitched shouts from the yard: 'Signora! Signora! Where are you?'

Betty ran to the top of the wooden steps. The diminutive Antonio stood in the middle of the yard, his small beady eyes darting hither and thither. Normally pinched and pale, he was now red-faced and breathless with excitement.

His mother shot out of the kitchen door. 'Whatever is the matter now, child?'

Antonio did not even hear her. As Betty emerged from the loft he ran up the steps and clasped her by the hand. 'Signora, there are Englishmen, many of them.'

'*Accidenti*! Keep your voice down, for the love of God,' his mother ordered, greatly alarmed. 'Do you want the whole village to hear?'

As her children clustered around them Betty ran her fingers through the boy's sparse hair and quietly asked, 'Where are the Englishmen, Antonio?'

'In the wood, Signora. Up there.' He pointed.

'How many?' Enrico asked.

'*Tanti*! *Tanti*!'

Betty wondered if the child had stumbled upon a partisan band. 'Could you count on your fingers, Antonio, do you think?'

Antonio screwed up his forehead and tried to visualise the men he had discovered. '*Uno*, *due*, *tre* ... It's difficult to remember, Signora, but there must have been ten anyway.'

Betty smiled gently. 'What were they doing?'

'Oh, you should see. It's marvellous, I tell you.'

'God give me patience,' sighed Piera. 'What is marvellous, for pity's sake?' In her voice exasperation blended with fear.

'They've made themselves a house. You never saw such a house. It's all hidden by leaves and branches. Marvellous!'

'How did you find them?' Betty asked.

'I heard the sound of an axe. I thought it might be Giorgio.'

'Giorgio is a relation of ours,' Piera explained. 'He's a guardian of

the woods. The Conte helped him to get the job. Did you know, Signora?'
'I do recall something,' Betty murmured.
'But it wasn't Giorgio,' Antonio went on. 'It was one of these Englishmen. Do you want me to show you their house, Signora?'
'I want to see it,' Billy cried.
'So do I,' said Teresa.
'I'm sure we all do,' Betty said, 'but I don't think we should all go at once. It would be best if Antonio took me alone the first time.'
'Oh, what a swizz!' Billy protested. 'Why shouldn't I come too? I'm Antonio's friend.'
'So am I,' said Teresa.
'You're only a girl.'
Teresa put her tongue out at him. 'Don't be swinish, Billy.'
'Shut up you two and listen to me,' Betty ordered. 'What matters more than anything else is that we shouldn't give away their hiding place. If a great horde of us goes up there, we may do just that. Besides, we don't want to draw attention to ourselves either. Remember, we're strangers here too, and if the Germans or fascists hear about us we may never meet the Englishmen at all.'
At that moment Domenico Bussoni came into the yard. Antonio ran over to his father and poured out the story of the Englishmen and their house in the woods.
Betty would have liked to take Enrico with her, but she knew that to do so would provoke a jealous outcry from her younger children.
She felt a tug at her sleeve. 'Let's go,' Antonio said impatiently.
'Do you mind if he takes me?' Betty asked Domenico.
'He's the only one who knows where they are, isn't he?'
'Thank you. I'll take great care of him.'
The other children watched enviously as the little boy led her out of the village and up the hillside.

When they first entered the wood, the pines were wide enough apart to allow them to go on walking side by side, but as they penetrated deeper the trees grew closer together and Betty dropped behind her small guide. The undergrowth also thickened, and brambles tore at her skirt as she struggled to keep up with him. Certainly, only people seeking a secure hiding place would have chosen such a dense plantation.
Every so often Antonio would pause to get his bearings, but he seemed to have an innate sense of direction, perhaps because he had gone with his grandfather to these woods ever since he could remember. They had been clawing their way forward for about twenty

minutes when Antonio halted. 'Can you hear anything, Signora?' he whispered.

Betty strained her ears, but all was still, so still that it seemed appropriate to whisper back. 'No, can you?'

'We are getting close. Shall I go and tell them I have brought you?'

'Need you do that, Antonio? Can't we just arrive together?'

The little boy opened his narrow, slit-like eyes as wide as they would go and looked at her. 'Well, when I found them earlier, one of the Englishmen had no clothes on.'

Betty tried not to look amused. 'Oh, I see. Perhaps you had better warn them I'm here, then,' she said, deferring to Antonio's modesty on her behalf.

'Wait here, Signora. I shan't be long.' He plunged confidently into the undergrowth once more.

Betty found a clear space where a tree had been felled and sat down on the stump. She wondered if it was her fellow countrymen who had cut it down for building material. It was utterly still in the wood until above her head a pigeon suddenly took flight with a flurry of wings. The silence descended again. Betty hoped fervently that Antonio really knew where he had led her and that they were not now both separated and lost. Could it all be a fantasy dreamed up by the child's vivid imagination? Guiltily, she remembered her promise to his father to take the utmost care of him. And now she had let him go off on his own even deeper into this jungle.

She looked back to see if they had left any tracks, but the undergrowth seemed to have closed in behind them. She listened intently again, but could hear nothing.

Another ten minutes passed and Betty was becoming increasingly worried when she thought she heard something from the direction in which Antonio had set off. A moment later came the unmistakable sound of undergrowth being trampled. Betty got to her feet and hid behind a thicket – just in case.

Peering round a thorn bush, she spotted Antonio advancing between the trees, followed by a lean muscular young man with a red beard, wearing a tattered greenish shirt and khaki drill trousers. As she was about to emerge from the thicket, the boy halted, looking puzzled, and shouted, 'Signora! Where are you?'

'Bravo, Antonio!' she shouted back, relieved and delighted. 'Bravo!'

He ran forward, then stopped and pointed proudly behind him. '*Ecco, uno degli inglesi.*'

'Doctor Livingstone, I presume,' Betty said with a smile.

The young man looked flabbergasted. 'So ye really are British. Ah didna believe it. Thought yon bairn was ha'en me on.'

Betty laughed. 'No need to ask where you come from.'

'Aye, Glasgy. An ah wish to Christ ah were there the noo.'

'Oh, I don't know. It would probably be raining.'

'Weel, what are you dae'in here, for heaven's sake?'

'Don't you think I should meet your friends?' Betty suggested. 'Then we could all swap stories.'

'Aye, mebbe we should. The lads are fair bursting oot of their skins wi' curiosity, I can tell ye. What would be your name, lady?'

'I'm Betty – Betty Marzano. My husband's Italian. What's yours?'

'I'm Fairgus. Pleased to meet you, Betty.'

'The pleasure's mine, Fergus.' Indeed, although she spoke lightly, she was profoundly moved. For the first time since they had left Spoleto she felt that she and her children were no longer alone in a hostile world.

Antonio was hopping about impatiently. '*Venite trovare gli altri.*'

'What's he saying?' Fergus asked.

'He wants us to go and find the others.'

'Aye, he's reet. C'mon, then.' Fergus led the way into the undergrowth. 'Ah dinna ken how the wee bairn found us in the first place.'

'He heard someone using an axe. He thought it was a cousin of his called Giorgio, who's a guardian of the woods.'

'Och aye, we've met yon Giorgio. There's naught the matter wi' him. He'd no betray us.'

'They're not a bad family, but very poor. My children and I are living in his uncle's loft in Roselli.'

'Ye have children, then?'

'Yes, four.'

'Lordy! How dae ye manage?' Fergus sounded appalled.

Betty laughed. 'Like you do, I suppose. The best we can.'

'Aye, but we've nae bairns. Ye speak their lingo, though. Ah suppose that's a help.'

Antonio, who had run on ahead, suddenly stopped and pointed. '*Ecco la casa, Signora. Guarda! Guarda!*'

A small circle of about twelve metres in diameter had been cleared and in the centre stood the wood cabin. The trunks of the trees felled to make the clearing had been used for its main structure, and the bigger branches for the roof. Other branches and foliage had been lashed to the framework to provide the walls. It looked solid and fairly rain-proof.

Five bronzed men were sitting in a patch of sunlight, stripped to the waist. When they heard Antonio's excited shout, they scrambled to their feet and stared with open curiosity at Betty, who smiled at them and said 'What a splendid house! Antonio told us it was marvellous and he was quite right.'

'You see, lads, the wee boy was no fibbing,' Fergus said. 'The lady *is* British. And she has four bairns of her ain. How do ye like that?'

The five men shuffled their feet but did not speak.

'Well, dinna gawp at the lassie like savages,' Fergus roared. 'Come and be introduced like Christians.'

They grinned sheepishly and edged forward.

'This is Hamish.' Fergus indicated a stocky young man of about twenty-five. 'He's ma pal. We shinned off together. Meet Betty. Ah've forgotten her surname, ah'm afraid.'

Betty felt her hand squeezed in an agonising grip and winced.

'Watch it, Hamish, you big bear,' Fergus warned him. 'He does'ny ken his ain strength.'

'You are all escaped P.O.W.s, aren't you?' Betty asked.

'Yes, we all got out of a stinking camp at a place called Pissignano, after the Ities packed it in.'

'Oh, Pissignano is near Spoleto, my home town, but I've never been there.'

'Ye've no missed anything,' Hamish growled.

'What are you doing in these parts, Missis?' A thin rather melancholy looking man spoke for the first time. 'My name's Rhodes, by the way. They call me Dusty.'

'I heard that the *Podesta* of Spoleto, that's the Mayor, planned to string us all up from five lamp-posts. But please don't mention that to my children, when you meet them. I haven't told them the grisly details.'

'Proper bastards, they fascists are, an' all,' said a dark boy with a slight stoop. 'Oh, I'm Alf Coles at your service. The dizzy blond over there is Jack, and that ancient Briton is Fred.'

'Watch it, cheeky,' said Fred, whose thinning hair did make him look considerably older than the others. He turned to Betty with a smile. 'I must apologise for our Alf. He's got no manners, even in the presence of a lady. I cook for these layabouts when there's anything to cook, but I'd be only too pleased to hand over to you.'

'How do you get on for food?' Betty asked.

'Oh, we go scrounging in twos or threes,' Fred answered. 'The people are pretty generous hereabouts, but they haven't much themselves, poor folk. I reckon we do fairly well, considering.'

'I wuidna' say no to a big bowl o' begoo,' Fergus said, licking his lips.

'What's begoo?' Betty asked.

'Porridge, Betty. When we were in the Western Desert wi' the Black Watch, wi' the 51st Highland Division, ye ken, they dished it up for brakefast every morning.'

'Have a heart, Fairgus,' Hamish begged, 'you're making my mouth water.'

Looking round at them, Betty saw that they were all very thin, even a normally burly pair like Fergus and Hamish. She noticed that several of them had sores on their legs where scratches had gone septic.

'We sometimes try to help the farmers in the fields,' Dusty said, 'but the slightest effort seems to make us bloody tired.'

She could see that none of them could stand much work. A year or more in prison, followed by a fortnight's semi-starvation, had not helped to build up their constitutions after the stress of battle and capture.

'We generally only sleep here,' Fred explained. 'We've found a broken-down old hut in a field, nearer Roselli. There's a good all-round view, so you can see anyone coming, and you can get down to the river to bathe or wash.'

'How do you pass the time when you're not looking for food?' Betty asked.

Jack, the fair boy, answered. 'We get pretty bored. We had to leave everything we had behind in the camp. Fred has got an old pack of cards, so sometimes we play whist or rummy.'

'It's not so bad on fine days,' Dusty added. 'You can sit in the sun, bathe or roam the woods, but it's not a lot of fun when it rains.'

Betty could imagine their discomfort, with the chilly wind of autumn already whistling down from the hills.

'Perhaps we could scrounge for food together sometimes,' she suggested. 'My boys speak Italian, of course, and one of us could go with one or two of you.'

The men brightened up at once.

'That's a fine idea, Betty,' Fergus said with a wide grin, 'and since ah was the lucky mon who brought you here, ah hope to hae the honour of being your first escort.'

'Ye'll needs take me along too as a chaperone,' Hamish added.

'Gooseberry more like,' Fergus growled.

Antonio, who had been admiring the log cabin, reappeared and began shuffling his feet again impatiently.

'I'd better go, or they'll be thinking we are lost,' Betty said.

'I'll come wi' ye and show you yon hut in the field,' Hamish said.

On the way back the Scotsman pointed out how they had marked trees unobtrusively to lead them through the wood to the cabin. But Antonio had no need of any aids to direction and walked boldly ahead of them.

When they emerged from the wood Hamish took the lead and guided them across country to the delapidated hut in the field which they had made their day headquarters. Betty could see that it was strategically well placed for a quick getaway, for quite near a precipitous path dropped steeply into a gulley that wound down from the hills. At the bottom the brambles and willows along the stream gave good protection, and where the water widened into a series of small pools the men could bathe and wash their tattered clothes.

Hamish walked part of the way with them, but when they came

within sight of Roselli he turned back towards the woods with a cheerful 'Be seeing ye again tomorrow, Betty.'

The children, who had been awaiting her return eagerly, plied her with questions. She had to describe the wood cabin and each of the prisoners in turn and what they had all said.

'When can we meet them, Mum?'

'Hamish suggested tomorrow.'

'Oh good! Good!'

In Piera's house the pasta was being kneaded and rolled out over and over again for supper, the main meal of the day. The peasants sat at one end of the table and Betty and her children at the other.

The only light came from a miner's lantern hanging from a beam. It lit up the table and the faces around, but served to make the rest of the room darker and more mysterious than ever. Betty never really discovered what was in it. In the corners were dark shapes that looked, by the smoke and dirt, as if they had been there for years. Broken-down cupboards and bulging sacks, strange instruments hanging on the walls, by age and disuse all had taken on the colour of dust, defying their curiosity and adding to the sense of melancholy that the house always inspired.

At this meal the peasants relaxed and really got down to their food, which was always *pasta asciutta*. As it was the one proper meal of the day, each had his own plate and fork and was served from the large dish in the middle. After the pasta came bread and wine and sometimes fruit.

Neighbours drifted in: Giuseppe, the hatchet-faced youth from next door who was looked on as an authority on world affairs; Mimma and her two pretty daughters; a crony of Domenico's from the mines; and a strange old man who always remained sitting stolidly on a stool before the fire the whole evening, never uttering, but staring slowly round the company with bleary eyes.

After supper the plates were heaped in a bucket and left to soak while everyone clustered round the fire, some sitting on benches, others standing leaning against the wall while the children squeezed into the huge fireplace, sitting grimy amongst the embers, listening entranced to the grown-ups' talk. No child ever went to bed before his parents, and sometimes little Silvana would drop off to sleep as she sat, with her head between her knees and her toes in the ashes.

Betty and her family went to bed in the dark, but later there was an air raid on Perugia and Foligno and they watched from their window. It was spectacular and far enough away to appreciate without the feeling that a stray bomb might fall on them by mistake. The raid went on for some time as several waves of aircraft passed over the target. Then it stopped as suddenly as it had started, and in the complete silence that ensued, out of the darkness somewhere below them, came a loud harsh voice:

'Ha! Just the job!'

They looked at each other in delight. The expression was unfamiliar then; how absurd and inadequate, yet how satisfactory! So from that moment, this snatch of Eighth Army slang passed into the family vocabulary.

The next day they made the acquaintance of several more escaped prisoners. Somehow the word had gone round that an Englishwoman was in Roselli and all day long there seemed to be figures in khaki lurking on the outskirts of the village, waiting to have a chat.

There were the two Reggies, who lived in a cave near the road to San Severo. Reggie I had been very ill and Betty asked him how he had got on for food.

'Well, I generally had more than I could manage. All the women round here made little dishes for me. There was a continual procession carrying little pots and packets which they placed among the bushes at the entrance to the cave. Some of them came right in and insisted on standing over me as I ate. It was a bit embarrassing sometimes when I had no appetite.'

He shook his head and sighed, but Betty could see by his expression that he was moved and grateful to the women who had insisted on his eating.

Reggie II was a butcher and one day Betty found him sitting on their doorstep with a large bundle in his arms.

'Here, take this,' he said and disappeared.

'This' was half a lamb, and they ate it that evening with relish. It was fine to eat meat again and to feel really full after a meal and they all went to bed thoroughly pleased with themselves and with life.

Next day, however, they met Carlo, the shepherd, whose flock was grazing further up in the hills.

'I don't know what's happening,' he complained, 'but the animals seem to be disappearing one after the other, especially the lambs. It's too early for the foxes. I can't understand it.'

'Most mysterious,' Betty murmured, feeling acutely embarrassed. She hoped that Piera, who had seen them cook and eat the meat, would not mention it.

Soon they knew all the prisoners and where they lived in stables, shacks, barns and caves. They all had some characteristic to remember them by and each child's face would light up at the sight of one of his favourites.

Enrico loved Fergus and Hamish because they were strong and fearless and treated him like one of themselves.

'Come on Enrico, lad,' Fergus would say, 'Gi' us a hand wi' yon tree trunk.'

Dusty and Fred played whist with Alec and Billy, and Alf proved to be a champion at conkers, though he made sure that Billy won his fair share of their matches.

Leslie, who had acquired a *casetta* on the hillside, was a shoemaker and mended Enrico's clogs for him. He shared his hut with Charlie, who had served in India before the war and hadn't been home for twelve years. He told the boys fascinating stories of monsoons and riots, polo and pig-sticking. Billy's favourite was Joe, who could carve life-like animals and figures out of bits of wood.

Teresa loved Jack because he had beautiful ash-blond hair, very thick, which she liked to stroke.

One day Giuseppe sidled up to Betty after breakfast. 'I hear Panella has a sick young Englishman in his stable,' he whispered.

Panella lived at San Severo, a hamlet about a mile away, and was known as one of the staunchest anti-fascists in the district. Later he was to be imprisoned for being too outspoken in his views.

Teresa, who had overheard Giuseppe's whisper, suggested that they should go and visit the sick soldier. Betty agreed and they left the boys playing with Fergus, Hamish and their band in the hut overlooking the river.

Having arrived at the village, they were asking the way to Panella's house when a khaki figure suddenly burst through a hedge and planted himself before Teresa, exclaiming ecstatically: 'Och, a wee lass in a kilt!'

Looking down, Betty saw that Teresa was wearing her old skirt of Macintosh tartan, to which she had no right at all. However, it pleased old Mac, who immediately picked her up and put her on his shoulder, to Teresa's great delight.

They marched triumphantly into Panella's stable where a bed had been placed far enough from the cows to allow a cane chair and a table to form a cosy corner round it, with a mirror hung on a nail.

'You're a lucky lad, George,' Mac announced. 'Here are two bonny lassies come to visit you.'

On the bed lay a pallid youth, George from Yorkshire, who had been laid low with a bad attack of jaundice. His faithful attendant, McFee, was a much older man who looked after his young friend with complete and touching devotion, bearing with patience and cheerfulness the invalid's frequent querulous moods.

'George had just gone down with the jaundice when we escaped together frae the camp. We walked all day and he passed oot, poor lad, just outside this village. Panella took us into his house and gave George the best bedroom.'

'Aye, the last thing I expected was for the Ities to treat us like that,' George said. 'In North Africa they was right bastards.'

'Nearly all the peasants are good people,' Betty told him.

'Elvira, the daughter of the hoose, looked after him until he was on the mend,' McFee explained, 'but now, for safety's sake, we've shifted him to this stable – I sleep in yon manger, and nice and warm it is too, with the old coos nuzzling me feet. That second door there gives straight on to the woods.'

Lying in bed, the poor boy was bored to tears, and as Betty sat and chatted to him the germ of an idea was born. Why shouldn't one of them go down to Spoleto and collect a few English books? She had plenty at Casa San Marzano, including novels, and she turned the scheme over in her mind as they walked home.

Next day she started making inquiries and found that at least one person from the village went down to Spoleto every day, generally by pony trap, and did commissions for anyone in Roselli who needed something.

As she usually did with any new scheme, she decided to consult Enrico as to which of them should go. 'I can't go myself. I'm too well known.'

'I'll go, Mum, like a shot.'

Betty thought for a moment. 'I daren't risk it, Enrico. You're too big. The fascists might grab you.'

'I'm much too young,' Enrico pointed out.

'I know you are, darling. But the black-shirts don't pay much attention to actual age. Seeing a well-grown boy like you, they might easily seize you and pack you off without saying a word to anyone.'

'There's only Alec, then, isn't there. Do you think he could manage, Mum?'

Betty thought he could. Alec was shrewd, and she knew he would be equal to any situation. When they called him in and put it to him, he was delighted at the prospect of a trip to town, and in his old ragged shirt he really looked like a peasant's son.

It transpired that Agnese, from next door, was going into town the following day, so at dawn they set off together. It was a long chilly journey sitting in an open trap, for the first frosts had come and the cold in these hills is intense during winter.

Alec jumped down from the trap just before they entered Spoleto, opposite the hospital, and cut across the fields past Ciacco's house. He knew Ciacco's two sons, who were always at loggerheads, and as usual sounds of squabbling were coming from the windows. Peeping in, Alec saw Luigi and Pietro hard at work pummelling each other, with their mother darting in and out squealing and poking each of the boys with a pointed stick. In the old days Alec would probably have joined in the mêlée but now, bearing in mind the injunctions of his mother and elder brother not on any account to make his presence known, he ran past the house, the yells getting fainter as he climbed up the hill through the olive groves.

It was mid-morning when he arrived at his home and made a careful reconnaissance to make sure no strangers were about before nipping into Giulia's house to glean the latest news.

The peasants were overjoyed to see him, having been sure the fascists had caught the whole family.

Serafina was there too. 'Oh, Alecky, what a fright I had after you left! Two fascists came to the house and asked for your Mamma. Oh, they were not good men and they were bristling with guns.'

Alec's eyes opened wide. 'What did you do?'

'Well, Elena was with me at the time and Pierino came into the courtyard too, so I wasn't alone. I told them your Mamma had gone to Rome with the whole family. They asked the address, but I pretended to be very stupid and didn't answer.'

Alec smiled, visualising the scene. Though Serafina was cunning and, alas, often light-fingered, she could play the 'idiot girl' brilliantly when she wanted to. Alec could well imagine the exasperation of the militiamen as they tried to get information out of her.

'Eventually the men went away, very annoyed about everything, but I don't think they'll return,' Serafina concluded.

Alec learned from Giulia that Serafina and Elena were living alone in Casa San Marzano and having the time of their lives, asking their friends in to dance to Betty's wireless and drink her wine. But at least they were able to keep an eye on things and inhabit the place so that it was not requisitioned.

At that moment, to Alec's great joy, Marcello Cimicchi appeared.

'Whatever are you doing here?'

'Come to feed the rabbits. I come every day and generally pop in for a chat with Giulia.'

The two boys were delighted to be together again and went off to brood lovingly over the rabbits, which were their special hobby.

After giving them a huge feed to celebrate the occasion, Alec asked Marcello to help him prepare the swag for his return journey. He put twenty or thirty English books, mainly Penguins, into a sack and then clambered up to the roof where his mother had hidden the daggers, which he very much wanted to retrieve. He also rooted out all the maps of Italy and the district, and various articles of clothing which he had been told by his brothers and sister to be sure to bring. All this made a large bundle.

Marcello carried the portable gramophone with some old dance records of the 'twenties, Alec humped the sack, and after saying goodbye to the peasants and Serafina the boys set off for Alec's rendezvous near the hospital. There they waited behind a hedge until they heard the pony's hooves and, peering out, saw the trap coming.

The stuff was loaded on and covered, as far as possible, with a large bundle of fodder and the various purchases Agnese had made, but the return journey was uneventful and that evening Betty was able to dole out books to the men and the gramophone screeched till late at night in Piera's kitchen.

Alec's venture had made them all hungry for contact with the outside world.

After supper next evening Betty said: 'What a pity there's no electric current in Roselli. Otherwise, we might get hold of our wireless and hear the news.'

It was maddening not to know where the Allies were, whether they were still advancing, whether they had taken Naples.

'But Giovanni has a wireless,' Piera said.

'Who's Giovanni?'

'You've seen that small newish house on the edge of the village?' Betty nodded. 'Well, Giovanni lives there. He owns a lot of the woods and he has electric current in his house because the mill which is next door has electric light.'

'Do you think he would mind if we went and listened?'

'You can but try. He's no fascist.'

By now is was nearly 9 p.m., so they went along to the smart little cottage they had already noticed. It was very dark, raining and miserable, and they stumbled on stones and into puddles in the pitch blackness.

On arriving they found the house silent and shut, but they knocked on the door and, as they did so, a dark form suddenly appeared beside them on the doorstep. The door was opened a crack and in the dim beam they saw several shadows detach themselves from the darkness and creep towards the light.

It was strange and eerie. Not a word was said. They pushed through the door and in the half light of the passage saw who it was who had accompanied them: a prisoner. And the others squeezing through the door in silence wore the familiar ragged khaki. A room on the right seemed full of people and they heard a quiet voice, so they peeped in.

A wireless stood on a table in the middle of a small whitewashed kitchen. Near the fireplace an old woman was knitting and round the room were rows of Anglo-Saxon faces, all with the same intent look, gazing towards the wireless and listening, listening to the subdued English voice that spoke to them of Allied victories, of hope, of liberation, of home.

Betty and her children stood in a corner and when the bulletin was over she went over to the only Italian in the room. Giovanni had a pleasant face and wore a curious fur cap like a drowned rat. In the weeks to come they never saw him without the cap, whether he was chopping wood in his shirtsleeves, eating his evening meal or dressed in his best to go to Spoleto. Did the cap conceal a bald head or some disfiguring mark, or was it just habit that made him wear it always? Anyway, he seemed friendly enough and said they could come when they liked to hear the news.

Then Betty turned to speak to some of the prisoners, but a tall fair boy warned: 'Ole Ma doesn't like us to stay here a moment after we've heard the news, so let's go outside and talk there.'

Indeed, the old woman was already showing signs of agitation and obviously wanted the room cleared. It was a very dangerous thing that Giovanni did, and small wonder the old girl had the jitters. If anyone in the village had chosen to play the spy, the whole lot would have been caught red-handed and Giovanni would have been charged with listening to Radio Londra and harbouring prisoners.

They all crept out, one by one, and forgathered in Giovanni's barn, where they talked and talked. Betty learned the names and histories of a dozen men whose faces she couldn't see and whose forms were darker blurs in the thick darkness, but their vibrant voices, against the soft hissing background of rain, told so much of themselves that sight seemed almost superfluous.

They sat far into the night and Teresa lay sleeping in Betty's lap, while Billy, sitting in the manger, leant heavily against his mother, drowsily enjoying the conversation. At last they broke away and some of the men accompanied them to Piera's door, one of them carrying Teresa in his arms. Then they all dispersed to their hiding places.

A few days later old Sabatino caught a chill in the mountains. It quickly turned to pneumonia, he retired to bed, and the next day was seriously ill. A doctor was called from San Giovanni, but by evening the old man was fighting for his life.

Betty kept her family out of the way as much as possible. They spent the whole day with the prisoners in the woods, but after dark they returned to their loft.

There was an atmosphere of melancholy about the place. They sat on their blankets, listening to the murmurs of the watchers around the sickbed below. At midnight the old man died and the house was filled with wailing.

They had had little to do with him, but he had seemed a pleasant old fellow, and strong. They were sorry, particularly for his wife, Carrera, who had welcomed them so warmly on that first night and had been friendly ever since. Everything was rather depressing for the children, however, so they went off to the woods very early, returning at midday to attend the funeral.

The coffin arrived in the afternoon and the old man was laid in it and carried down the steps. The door was very narrow and there was some jostling and bickering as they tried to get it through. Eventually the procession was formed, with Domenico and Giuseppe carrying the coffin, followed by Carrera and the rest of the family, most of the villagers and some of the prisoners who had helped Sabatino with his wood-cutting.

The cemetery was off the road to San Severo, about a quarter of a mile from the village, but as the procession, headed by the priest, rounded a corner a small boy came running along the road towards them:

'Fascists! Fascists! Coming up the valley!'

Domenico and Giuseppe dumped the coffin in the middle of the road and made off across a field that led to the woods. The prisoners pushed through the hedge and ran down the steep slope to the stream. The panic was catching and the others turned tail hastily towards the village, some to warn the young men and the prisoners, others to find hiding places for their valuables, knowing that the fascists were not above laying their hands on anything they fancied during their raids.

The coffin sat in the middle of the road, poor old Carrera, heedless of the tumult, kneeling in the dust beside it, and the priest standing impatiently nearby. All the dogs were barking furiously.

Fergus and Hamish, who were sitting in Piera's kitchen awaiting Betty's return, sprang through the window on to the dungheap, sinking up to their knees in muck, and, plunging out, ran off into the woods. Betty hid Enrico in a recess off the stable camouflaged with firewood. Presently all was quiet, the women sitting innocently knitting at their doors, the dogs lying in the sun, snapping occasionally at flies, and still the coffin lay in the road with the kneeling figure bowed over it, and the priest waited.

Half an hour passed, an hour, with no sign of fascists or anyone else, and they realised it had been a false alarm.

People began to creep back, rather shamefaced, to the funeral. Domenico and Giuseppe picked up poor old Sabatino, who was borne to his last resting place without further interruption.

After this scare Betty decided they must have some sort of danger signal to warn the men up in the woods not to come down into the village. The loft window faced the mountainside, the woods and the ravine where most of the prisoners were hiding. They were discussing it with Fergus, Hamish and the others, lying on the grass outside the derelict hut.

'How aboot a towel?' Fergus suggested.

'We only have one between us,' Betty pointed out, 'and someone might be using it when we need it.'

Her fingers were playing idly in the grass and, looking down, she saw that she had a convolvulus plant in her hand. The sight of it awakened some memory, but she couldn't recall exactly what. At the same instant a thought occurred to Billy.

'Mummy, the convolvulus, doesn't that suggest something?'

'Of course! Our lovely *vaso*.'

'Well, put that on the windowsill. It's so white and shining you could see it for miles.'

When they explained that a *vaso da notte* meant a chamber-pot, and what a splendid specimen they themselves possessed, the prisoners roared with laughter.

'You're a right wee genius, Billy lad,' Fergus said.

So the *vaso* came into its own, fulfilling a more exalted role than its normal one.

Alas for the best laid plans.

Cleaning out the loft next morning, Betty as usual placed the basin and other objects on the windowsill out of the way. Later she prepared a meal for the men which they carried to the field by the walnut tree, but after waiting some time they saw no sign of the prisoners. Finally, overcome by hunger, they ate their own soup and returned sadly to the house.

Not a soul came to the village that day, so in the evening Betty decided to send Enrico and Alec up into the woods to see what had happened to all their friends. They arrived to find the men hiding.

'Is it all clear?' Hamish asked.

'What do you mean, all clear?'

'Well, the danger signal has been out since morning. We reckoned the fascists were searching the village. We've bin worrying oorselves silly for a' of ye.'

Yes, there was the *vaso*, on the windowsill where Betty had forgetfully left it that morning, a signal and a warning to everyone.

Betty seldom allowed herself the luxury of introspection but that night she lay awake thinking of their life during the last year or two and of their extraordinary existence at Roselli now. She thought first of Valentino, of course, but firmly put him out of her mind, guessing that he might have joined the partisans after the Italian Armistice and knowing that if he had he would be in even greater danger than they were themselves. She had enough problems of her own, she told herself, without imagining horrors for her husband.

The children had adapted themselves marvellously quickly to their strange new life, half peasant, half refugee. She still played games with them, but there was no call for cowboys and Indians with the real enemy so menacing and so close at hand.

Since they had been at Roselli, however, they had not set eyes on a single German or fascist. Betty did the best she could to make the enemy's image less frightening. She drew pictures of bovine-looking Germans having their rifles pinched by agile partisans, of comic-opera fascists like the ones who had scared Serafina at Colle Attivoli, of Colonello Boldoni stamping on his hat with rage.

At Betty's prompting, the prisoners put on little plays in which Fred, Dusty and Jack were cast as gormless Germans who were invariably routed by the children's partisan band led by Fergus and Hamish. The prisoners seemed to enjoy this make-believe, interspersed with games of whist, rummy, Old Maid and a variation of Happy Families, as much as the children did.

The main problem, of course, was food, as it had been since 1941, when rationing was introduced a year after Italy came into the war. They got their rations monthly, or were supposed to, but sometimes those rations had to last for six months, sometimes for two, and this made it difficult to know how much to allocate for a given period. Most of the time they had no sugar, never any butter or margarine, no tea or coffee, no jam, no soap, meat every four months, and no fish.

Indeed, throughout the war, they lived almost entirely on vegetable soup, varied according to the seasons, and usually with a handful of macaroni or rice cooked with it. Then they had salad, often going into the fields to gather leaves and plants that the peasants had taught them to recognise. There was a wide variety of these, used only by the country folk, and with a drop from their tiny ration of olive oil and a dash of vinegar, they made a very tasty dish.

Sometimes they got eggs, and often home-made cheese, though little or no milk. But up here at Roselli they considered themselves well off because Beppe the miller sold them, at a fair price, almost as much flour as they needed, so they had abundant bread for themselves and were also able to help the prisoners.

Sometimes they got maize-flour and made *polenta* with the peasants. The manner in which this was eaten was peculiar. The maize-flour, cooked in boiling water to the consistency of porridge, was poured straight on to the kitchen table which was usually, but not always, washed beforehand. The sticky stuff spread all over, getting slower as it cooled, until finally there was a stratum about half an inch thick. On to this was poured tomato sauce.

Meanwhile, the whole family had been standing round, spoon in hand, anxiously watching for the moment to begin. Then they fell on it, each one spooning up the bit in front of him. Naturally, the most dexterous got the lion's share. The children could eat out wondrous shapes of hats and castles, decked with bits of tomato sauce, so a meal like this provided entertainment as well as nourishment.

Their normal cooking arrangements were comic enough, Betty thought, smiling to herself in the dark. The peasants prepared all their food over the open fire, either in a huge cauldron hung on a hook over the flames or in earthenware jugs standing in the embers. At the San Giovanni market in Spoleto Betty had bought two of these earthenware jugs and all their food was prepared in them, tasting intriguingly of smoke, cinders and ash blown up by the various people who had fanned the fire to make it burn brighter, of soot falling from the chimney or the bottom of the cauldron, and faintly of all the previous messes cooked in the jug, for the earthenware seemed to have a retentive property as if everything cooked in it was stored away in the porous clay to be produced at all subsequent meals.

There was always a fight over the brightest embers, Piera's jugs and theirs jostling each other for the hottest patch. Sometimes the dish would take hours to cook, while the children brooded hungrily over it, and pushed bits of red wood against the jug in a vain effort to speed up the process. There was no way of cooking other than boiling. Piera did possess an iron frying pan, but it never semed to be used.

One day Piera came in looking very important: 'Signora, the Sergeant-Major to see you.'

Betty had heard a lot about this Sergeant-Major and felt honoured that such an exalted person should visit them. He was at least six foot five, she had been told. He spoke Italian well and spent all his time going round finding out where other prisoners were living and seeing if he could help them. He often covered miles in a day, walking from one village to another, seeking out his men.

Betty pulled her one old dress straight and ran down to receive the visitor. Outside the front door she found herself up against a high tower of shabby but clean and well pressed battledress. Craning her head upwards, her gaze encountered the owner's mild brown eyes.

'How do you do?' he spoke formally, as if they had just been introduced at a cocktail party.

'Very well, thank you,' Betty replied. 'Won't you come in?' Then, remembering that Piera had banned prisoners from the house, she added hastily, 'No, you can't come in, I'm afraid, but do take a seat,' indicating the top step.

With perfect manners the Sergeant-Major bent down, brushed some chicken droppings aside, laid out a ragged handkerchief and handed Betty to her seat, sitting down himself beside her.

'What's your name?' she asked. 'I can't call you Sergeant-Major.' For one thing, she thought, despite his imposing stature he was so unlike the daunting popular image of that rank.

'I should hope not. I'm Michael – Michael St. John. My Italian friends call me Michele, or San Giovanni, or sometimes even San Michele, which makes me feel like Axel Munthe. How I wish I was! Didn't you love that book?'

Betty guessed that he could not have made that joke before, since few of his fellow prisoners could be expected to have read *The Story of San Michele.*

'I've always wanted to ask someone called St. John why you pronounce it Sinj'n,' Betty said.

'I've no idea. Perhaps my ancestors wanted to disclaim any kinship with the Apostle. From what I know of them I'd say they weren't a particularly saintly lot.'

'The prisoners round here may not regard you as a saint, but they think very highly of you.'

Michael St. John made a deprecatory gesture. 'One has to tread very warily. Lads placed in the position they find themselves don't take kindly to authority, and I can't say I blame them. About all King's Regulations say about prisoners-of-war is that it's their duty to escape, and they've done that, haven't they?'

'But you spend all your time trying to help them, don't you?' Betty insisted.

Michael shrugged. 'There's pathetically little one can do. My Italian is generally a bit more fluent than theirs, so if they have any problems with the locals I can sometimes help to straighten them out. I wish I could get them out of khaki and dressed like peasants – we should all be much less conspicuous then – but since I haven't a hope in hell of finding any *contadino* gear that would fit me, I am hardly in a position to urge it on them.'

'Anyway,' Betty pointed out, 'the peasants in Umbria are mostly so poor that they wouldn't have any clothes to spare.'

'That's quite true. Further north they are much better off. Most of the prisoners I bumped into on the way down had found themselves civvies and melted into the landscape.'

'Where did you escape from?'

'A camp on the edge of Mantua. I probably should have had a go at Switzerland. It would have been much nearer.'

'Why didn't you?'

'Well, after the Armistice everyone said the Germans would get out of Italy. I wasn't so sure, but I did think our chaps would advance a lot faster than they have done. Also, if I made for the front I shouldn't have to cross any frontiers.'

'Are you going on down eventually?'

'I've decided to stay put for the moment. I was taken to see a member of the Italian National Liberation Committee the other day and he said this was the advice given to escaped prisoners. I've also heard that conditions near the front are pretty grisly.'

'You must have to steer well clear of the Germans,' Betty said. 'With your height you couldn't possibly pass for an Italian. How do you manage it?'

'I get around mainly by night, moonlit ones if possible. Good for the map-reading, if one has a map, or the astronomy, if one hasn't.' He looked down at her and smiled. 'But I refuse to waste a precious afternoon with a pretty girl talking of nothing but this wretched war. What was the last play you saw in London, Betty?'

She was startled, then delighted. '*French without Tears*, I think. Did you see it?'

Michael nodded. 'Rex Harrison was splendid, of course, but for me Roland Culver made the evening.'

'And Kay Hammond, surely, for a man?'

'She was gorgeous, yes. I love that voice, too.'

They talked of other plays and films they had seen, of the joys of London, of pictures and parties, books and places to dance. They sat in sight of the whole village, surrounded by filth and squalor, the future for both of them uncertain, and the incongruity of it all heightened their pleasure in the conversation.

Half an hour later, reverting to the present, Betty asked, 'Why aren't you an officer, Michael?'

'Well, they have offered me a place at an O.C.T.U. – twice, actually – once soon after I joined up as a private and again just before I got put in the bag in North Africa.'

'Why did you turn it down. I should have thought you were definitely "officer material" – isn't that what they call it?'

Michael's brown eyes twinkled. 'Ghastly expression, isn't it? Makes one sound like a piece of cloth. Mind you, some of them are! As for me, I'd come up the hard way, through the ranks. As a sergeant-major I was *someone*. Everyone knew me, and I saw a lot more of the game with the C.O. at Battalion H.Q. than I would have done as a second-lieutenant in command of a platoon, or even as a company commander, if I'd got that far. It was much more interesting.'

Betty could have gone on talking with him all day, but she felt a twinge of guilt. 'I'd better go and see what my children are up to.'

'Likewise mine,' Michael said with a wave towards the woods, 'but first I shall try to date you, as the Yanks would say. How about tomorrow?'

From that day they were constant companions and did all their scrounging in company. When they managed to get extra bread or cheese they prepared little parties in outlying farms, carrying the gramophone up there and some of the store of tea which Alec had dug up in the garden at Colle Attivoli.

Half a dozen of the prisoners would turn up, and the peasants would goodheartedly sit in the corners and leave their self-invited British guests the fireside and table, watching their every movement and evidently sharing their enjoyment.

The tealeaves were always put on a plate and dried for the next day. When the tea made from them got too weak they were used for cigarettes, and Betty would produce a fresh handful and boil it up in the earthenware pot, so about one day in four they had really black tea. Although they had no sugar, they found some curious stuff called fig honey, like black treacle only nastier, but at least it sweetened their tea and could be spread on bread.

These parties helped to keep them in good heart and the peasants often produced some wine – kept hidden away from the Germans.

After his first successful journey Betty sent Alec to the house at Colle Attivoli about once a week to fetch various things to make their loft at Roselli more comfortable.

In Piera's kitchen one evening Giuseppe, the foreign affairs expert, remarked: 'You know old Uncle Aldo has a really big cart that he takes to Spoleto now and then?'

'Big enough to carry beds?' Betty asked with interest.

'No problem.'

Betty had never got used to sleeping on the loft floor, which was extremely hard and uncomfortable. Whatever position she lay in, the bricks seemed to bore through the quilt beneath her in five minutes. Every morning she awoke with the feeling that she had been rolling on pointed flints all night.

When the beds duly arrived Fergus helped to put them up and there was great rejoicing, even though the boys had slept well enough on the hard floor. The loft looked quite adorned and that night Betty, revelling in her own soft mattress, slept soundly all night.

They also brought up the wireless, hidden in a bale of hay, and got permission to put it in Mimma's house because there seemed to be an electric wire running to the place from somewhere.

Three experts from among the prisoners, Jimmy, Fred and Nobby, were called in to fix the wireless. Mimma's house consisted of one room about six foot square and a loft above it where she slept with her two curvaceous daughters. When the three men and the wireless were all in the parlour there was not much elbow room.

'They seem to be taking a long time,' Betty said late in the afternoon. 'Go and see how they are getting on, Enrico.'

'They're very meticulous about everything,' he reported on his return.

Betty gave them another hour, then went to investigate for herself. As she approached the house she heard sounds of smothered giggling, but at first she could not make out why they were so reluctant to finish the job.

Mimma, a wrinkled little creature, sat in the chimney corner, knitting. Then, glancing up, Betty discerned two pairs of bright eyes peering out of the gloom. Looking closer, she saw that the two daughters were lying on the floor of the loft and gazing down through the trap door.

That evening the whole village crowded round the door and bulged into the room while Jimmy solemnly twiddled the knobs.

'This is London calling,' a voice intoned and the company held its breath. Suddenly there was a screeching, a grating and a prolonged quacking of ducks. Then the wireless went dead and no amount of coaxing produced so much as a squeak. The experts tried all next day, morally assisted by the charmers from the loft, but the wireless obstinately refused to emit another sound.

'May I borrow your bike please, Piera?' Alec asked at lunch next day.

'Off to Spoleto again?' Piera wagged her finger at him. 'You be careful, young man.'

'I haven't been for over a week and I'll be back before dark.'

'Is that a promise?' his mother put in.

'Of course, Mum. I can do the round trip in a couple of hours, and you know you need that pepper grinder from the house.'

The rest of the family and several of the prisoners decided to go to Paoletti's farm, where they had started the apple-picking. The trees grew in terraces down the hillside, old and gnarled but bearing an abundant crop which delighted the locals, who could look forward to plenty of apples that winter to supplement their meagre stores.

The apples were small and far from perfect, but glowed blood-red along the vista of old grey trees, paling in the hazy autumn distance. Many pickers were already at work, the khaki figures of the prisoners and the dull black dresses of the peasants making of the whole a lovely colour picture. Not for the first time Betty longed for her paints and for peace of mind to paint what she saw.

The pact seemed to be that they could all eat as much as they liked so long as they did a certain quota of work. Paoletti was kind. He knew that the prisoners were weak and likely to become exhausted before long. The apples were ripe and juicy and seemed like food from Paradise, so altogether there was more eating than working.

There was a lighthearted feeling in the air. The peasants sang as they worked, the women's shrill, hard voices trilling arias from *Butterfly* and *Rigoletto* with tuneful accuracy, while the prisoners, not to be outdone, sang popular or bawdy songs, 'Roll out the Barrel' or 'The Ball of Kirrimuir'.

Basket after basket was taken to the farm and weighed until finally Paoletti called them in for refreshment. Over wine the boys became loquacious. Fergus and Hamish refought the African campaigns with matches and apples and long, heated arguments about the relevant positions.

They sat on until after dark and in the back of her mind Betty was wondering if Alec was home, but when they got back to Piera's house there was no sign of him and she sensed the first tremors of anxiety. She wandered down the village to ask if anyone returning from Spoleto had seen him on the road.

'Oh yes,' said Agnese, who had been down that day by trap, 'I'm sure we passed him near San Giovanni, riding a bicycle. About two hours ago that was, so he ought to be here soon now.'

Betty remembered Alec's remark about the round trip taking only two hours. She didn't like the thought of his being out after dark, especially after curfew, for although there were no patrols in these remote villages, if he had been detained for some reason further down the road anything might have happened.

'I think I'll go and meet him,' she said casually, keeping the anxiety out of her voice.

Domenico, sometimes more sensitive than he appeared, offered to lend her his bicycle.

'I'll come too, Mum,' Enrico said.

Just as they were setting off they were joined by Antonio, his four-foot figure enveloped in an enormous hairy cloak which, with his naturally diabolical expression, made him look like a young Torquemada. It was a hazy moonlit night, very cold and silent, as if the world were holding its breath, and so still that they thought they could hear distant bombing.

They went on and on, expecting to see Alec at every turn, but the road always stretched ahead, gleaming and empty, beckoning them with the promise of the next bend. As they continued, mile after mile, a gnawing fear started to invade Betty, still buoyed up by the hope of seeing a solitary figure toiling up the road. But all was still and silent, the empty road mocking them and luring them on.

The mist hung in whisps now as they descended from the hills and presently they came to a few isolated farms. They knocked on one door but no one answered. They tried another, but still no reply. They knew there were people inside, for they could hear them, but in such bad times no one would open at night for fear of spies or Germans, and goodness knows what plotting or partisan meetings went on behind locked doors, especially in lonely farmhouses.

Alec reckoned he had made the trip to his old home in record time. The road to Spoleto was nearly all downhill and he even pedalled up part of the steep slope to Colle Attivoli. Apart from his promise to be back at Roselli before dark, he had a private reason for wanting to get there as soon as possible. He hoped to catch his friend Marcello feeding their rabbits again and to learn the latest gossip from him.

Sure enough, there was Marcello at the last hutch pushing in the remaining sprigs of greenery that he had brought. Serafina let them into the house and they sprawled in comfortable armchairs swapping their news. Time slipped by.

'Oh God.' Alec said, looking at his watch, 'I must go. I'm due back in Roselli in less than an hour.'

'You'll do it all right on a bike,' Marcello assured him.

Alec whizzed down the hill to Spoleto and pedalled frantically through the town. When he reached the suburbs on the other side he relaxed a little, but just before he got to San Giovanni his back tyre went flat.

'Whatever I do I shall be out after curfew now,' he thought. He hid in a hedge until it was dark and the road deserted, and then he started to tramp back to Spoleto, which was much nearer than Roselli, leaving the bicycle behind a hayrick whence he would retrieve it next day.

Soon he felt very tired and, seeing a vehicle coming towards him, stepped out to thumb a lift, but the car shot by. He tried several more but none stopped and he was in despair when a large truck slowed down at his sign.

Perhaps the driver felt sorry for the small dejected figure in the dimmed headlights, or perhaps he stopped out of curiosity, but Alec was seized by a large horny hand and hauled up into the driver's seat, where he found herself perched on the knees of an extremely dirty German mechanic.

The Germans were in good spirits, laughing and joking, and as Alec jumped down on the edge of Spoleto they pushed a cigarette and a slice of dark bread into his hand, never guessing who the boy was. Only pausing to light the cigarette, he climbed the hill to his home, lay down on the sofa and slept. Serafina seemed to have disappeared and there was no one else in the house.

Meanwhile, Betty and the two boys had at last reached the village of San Giovanni. After knocking at several houses they found someone, less suspicious or perhaps more innocent than the others, who opened up and, seeing their evident distress, invited them in. They told their story and asked if anyone had seen a little boy.

'We haven't seen him,' they answered, 'but why not telephone to your home in Spoleto? He might be there.'

'A marvellous idea, but have you got a telephone?' Betty asked, surprised to find one in such a humble dwelling.

'No, but we live next door to the post office.'

'Oh, I see,' said Betty with a tired smile. So while they prepared some wine for the unexpected visitors, she and Enrico picked the lock of the door which led through into the post office and telephoned.

After an age a cross and sleepy voice answered. Yes, it was Alec, and between yawns he recounted his adventures.

The relief of knowing he was safe was enormous, and they drank lightheartedly with their hosts till long after midnight before starting their long trek back to Roselli. It was mistier and more eerie than ever, with the green moonlight shimmering over everything.

They walked briskly, pushing the bicycle by turns. Betty and Enrico were singing softly when suddenly a figure loomed up out of the mist before them, then two or three more, grey and silent as ghosts.

They were German soldiers and they stopped in line abreast across the road, barring the way. As Betty peered more closely she saw that two of them were carrying a very large, very heavy bundle rolled in sacking slung from a pole. From the bundle slowly dripped something dark. Betty's hair stood on end and she felt the gooseflesh creep up her back. Enrico gave a horrified gasp while Antonio pressed closer to her.

The German before them opened his mouth to speak and it became a black cavern in his face. His eyes too were dark caves under his peaked hat. The only thought in Betty's consciousness was that in a moment they too might be a thing in sackcloth, oozing blood. She stood rigid, frozen with horror, but the soldier evidently decided they were not worth bothering about and had nothing worth looting. He barked a guttural word of command to the others, who moved forward, some on one side and some on the other, and they were swallowed up in the mist again, leaving Betty and the boys still standing transfixed on the lonely road.

'Mummy,' panted Enrico, 'did you see the body they had in the sacking?'

But commonsense came to Betty's rescue. 'Yes, I saw the body all right, but it was only a pig.'

'How do you know?' Enrico asked, looking immensely relieved nevertheless.

'Well, if they had killed someone they would hardly be dragging him for miles like that, would they? No, it must have been an unofficial piece of marauding, perhaps to supplement the sergeants' mess, because one of the other men had a chicken in his hand.'

They set off again. The bizarre encounter had dampened their spirits and they sang no more. It was a long way but a black cat followed them, just out of reach. If they stopped, he stopped; when they went on so did he, miaowing occasionally like a lost soul. Eventually Antonio caught him and wrapped him in the folds of his cloak where he settled down comfortably, except when attacked by nerves, indigestion or some other worry that made him claw convulsively at the boy's chest.

They felt the cat was a good omen. They decided to keep him as a mascot and call him Tip, as they had been singing 'Tipperary' when they met the Germans. He stayed with them for months but proved impossible to house train. No one's bed was sacred to him so finally he was given away.

Next morning who should arrive but Serafina.

'What on earth brings you here, Serafina *mia*?' Betty asked. 'I thought you preferred Spoleto.'

'Well, Signora, I quarrelled with Elena. She wanted to take some of your wine – you know, that good San Marzano wine – for a party. But she hadn't asked me to the party, so why should I let her take your wine? Now she's gone off in a huff and I hate being in the house alone.'

'Where will you sleep here?'

'Don't worry, I have an aunt and a cousin and I can share their bed.'

Serafina's family was amazing. The whole countryside seemed to be peopled with her relations, yet Serafina's parents had produced this, their only child, when they were both nearly fifty – exceptional for Italian peasants who start having their enormous families when they are about seventeen.

From subsequent conversations Betty gathered that the electrician had not come up to scratch, so Serafina's real reason for coming to Roselli was to nurse a broken heart, and, incidentally, to look out for someone else. But the broken heart did not seem to worry her much, and Betty and the children had all the glory of a maid to sweep their loft and cook their vegetable soup.

The life suited Serafina wonderfully. After flicking about in the loft for ten minutes and raising clouds of dust which settled impartially again on the beds or floor, while snatches of opera floated down, she would brush her hair with Betty's brush and saunter out to stand in the street for the rest of the day.

Looking about for someone to mend her broken heart, her eye fell on the hatchet-faced Giuseppe, their next door neighbour. He was a man of property, for he owned the hovel he lived in himself and also a stony patch of ground where, with a great deal of trouble, he managed to coax a few cabbages and beans to life.

Giuseppe was flattered by the attention of so comely a wench and soon the romance was in full swing. But it never really came to anything. Either Serafina decided that she could do better for herself elsewhere, or Giuseppe thought he would prefer a less flighty wife, for Serafina was bowled over by the prisoners and the sight of a khaki figure would send her into spasms of coyness.

Betty and the children spent hours sitting in the mill chatting with Beppe. This was partly because the miller was so garrulous that it was difficult to get away once they had called, but he was very good to them all. He gave a grand supper for them for which he killed a fatted goose, and they had so much to eat that they were all ill afterwards. He invited the men too, one or two at a time, and treated them just as grandly.

Betty once asked him why he did so much for the English prisoners. Before he could launch into one of his long philosophical dissertations, his wife answered:

'Because they are all mothers' sons; because they are good and kind in themselves. They are wonderful and never complain. They are in constant danger, homeless, hungry, yet they are always cheerful and ready to play with the children. Also,' she added with emphasis, 'they are so clean and well shaved.'

This in itself was a source of amazement to the Italian peasant, who considered shaving a Sunday luxury and liked his hair long and romantic, in contrast to the prisoners, who passed their one razor from hand to hand and trimmed each other's hair with nail scissors, never appearing in public until they were clean and tidy.

'And,' continued Mrs Beppe, 'we would like to think that if our own sons were in the same position over in England, the English mothers would be good to them, as we are to theirs.'

Thus spoke Beppe's wife, and it was the reply of thousands of poor women all over Italy, giving what they could to the hungry and homeless, without thought of nationality or creed, but just seeing a poor human being in need.

Betty was often struck by the widely varying and often contrasting attitudes taken by different men towards the war.

Going as usual to visit her prisoner friends in the hut above the river, she found them engaged in earnest conversation with two wild-looking creatures in shirts and wide-brimmed hats with several days' stubble on their faces. They were South Africans, passing through, and their urgency infected the others, who had hitherto been content to remain in Roselli, for months if necessary, until the Allies arrived.

But the South Africans were of a different calibre, and they spurned the thought of sitting down and waiting. They consented to stay two days. Then they would go on and try to cross the lines. They wanted the other men to join them.

Many and long were the arguments for and against. With the fighting traditions of a highland regiment behind them, Fergus and Hamish would almost certainly have joined the South Africans, Betty thought, but they had departed the previous day on an expedition to a distant village in search of food and they were not expected back until after the South Africans had gone on their way.

In the end Dusty Rhodes and the fair-haired lad, Jack, decided to go. Betty unearthed the daggers and maps that Alec had brought from Colle Attivoli. With her greater knowledge of the country she was able to help them plan their route, and this took the best part of a day. Next morning she and the children accompanied them down the road, kissing them all goodbye on the bridge and waving until they turned the bend in the road. Heartbroken at losing her beloved Jack, Teresa cried all the way home to the village.

They never heard how many got through, but a few weeks later Betty, Billy and Teresa were chatting with Beppe at the end of the village when they looked up and saw a familiar blond figure toiling up the road towards them. With a delighted cry of 'Jack!' Teresa tore up the road and flung herself into his arms. He embraced her fondly, but when he got closer they saw that his features were haggard with fatigue and he hardly had the strength to carry her.

With muttered expressions of astonishment Beppe took him gently by the arm and ushered them all into the mill house, where he quickly produced a loaf of bread, a flask of wine and a huge *prosciutto* (smoked ham), an unheard-of luxury at that time, from which he carved large slices and set them before Jack, who was so exhausted that he could only look down goggle-eyed at his plate. Before he could summon the energy to eat, Mrs Beppe came bustling in and carved more slices for Betty and the children.

The food and wine revived him slightly, but they did not press him for his story. Eventually, however, he gave a deep sigh and spoke for the first time.

'My God, Betty, it was awful, bloody awful!'

'Don't talk yet if you don't want to.'

'The cold, you've no idea. There's snow six foot deep on the mountains and bugger-all shelter. In the villages, such as they are and there aren't many, they don't dare take in prisoners any more. Jerry puts on raids all the time – I think he uses them to train the troops behind the lines – and if prisoners are found in a house the Italians sheltering them are shot out of hand.'

'Did you get anything to eat?'

'Precious little. They'd try to sneak you out something if they could, but they were scared stiff and I don't blame them.'

'Did you try to get through the lines?'

'Aye, we had to. More and more prisoners were arriving every day and nowhere for them to stay. But it was hopeless. With snow on the ground we left a great trail behind us and at night you didn't know where you were making for.'

'What happened?'

Jack passed a weary hand over his brow. 'I reckon we did fairly well – until Dusty stepped on a mine and blew his foot off. We'd had it then. Jerry heard and came and scooped us up.'

Beppe and his wife were craning forward, longing to know what Jack was saying. Betty quickly recounted his story so far in Italian.

'But how did he get back here?' Beppe asked, dumbfounded. For most Italians capture by the *tedeschi* was the end. Escape was outside their scheme of things.

'It was thanks to you I got away, Betty.' Jack said with a faint smile. 'They were front-line troops, the Jerries who recaptured us, you see, and they didn't make much of a job of searching us – not like the guards in the prison camp. That dagger you gave me was still in the bottom of my old pack and they never found it.'

Betty looked horrified. 'You don't mean to tell me you killed one of them with it.'

'Nothing as heroic as that, I'm afraid. They shoved us all in cattle trucks on a train bound for Germany. I had your dagger and another chap had a sort of home-made axe. We managed to cut a hole in the roof. We had to lie for what seemed like hours on top of the train until it slowed down going up into the mountains before crossing into Austria. Then we jumped for it. A Jerry guard at the back of the train saw us and opened fire. We ran like hell into some woods, but we got separated and I never saw the other bloke again. I reckoned I was better off with you all here than anywhere else in Italy and here I am – praise be to God!'

'What happened to the South Africans?'

'I don't know. We had to split up well before we reached the front-line area. No family could feed more than two at a time. After the four of us had been turned down twice, we agreed to make for different villages. I hope they made it.'

After they had eaten, Mrs Beppe made up a bed in the spare room where Jack could rest undisturbed for a while.

A few days later Betty was shown the other side of the coin.

She had gone down to fetch water from the fountain at the bottom of the village. She had put the *damigiana* under the jet of water and was waiting for it to fill when, looking up, she saw peering at her round the corner of the washhouse one of the most villainous faces she had ever seen. Presently a figure entirely in keeping with this face sidled into view, dressed in full fascist rig and carrying, Betty saw with alarm, a tommy-gun.

The creature leered at her and made signs, putting his fingers to his lips to enjoin secrecy, and two others loomed up behind him, of the same piratical appearance, lacking only knives between their teeth to complete the effect. They all gazed at each other, and to Betty's astonishment she realised that they were more frightened of her than she of them.

'Signora,' hissed the first, 'don't give us away.'

'What do you want?' Betty asked, still trembling slightly.

'We're fed up with this war, with the Germans, with the fascists. One doesn't get a moment's peace. So we've taken these' – patting the tommy-guns lovingly – 'and we've deserted from the black-shirts. We're looking for a hiding-place where we can live until the Allies come.'

'What will you live on?'

'We have arranged for our wives to come up here with food three times a week, so we'll be all right in hiding.'

'Why don't you join the partisans?'

'And have to fight? Not on your life. That's what we have come away from. We only want to hide in peace until the war's over.'

'Why don't you give those arms to the partisans, then? They'd be glad of them.'

'Oh, no. We're going to keep those ourselves and then we'll feel safe.'

Betty shrugged. 'Well, there are plenty of caves further up the mountain.'

Whereupon these heroes turned and disappeared into the bush. Later she saw them crawling slowly up the steep path, bowed down by the weight of their arms.

Despite Jack's unhappy experiences, many prisoners still passed through the village on their way south to try to cross the lines. All types and all nationalities were represented. Besides Frenchmen and Yugoslavs, several Russians hurried through at various times, their feet tied up in rags. Probably they had swapped their boots for food, but no one could understand them, their Italian being limited to a few words of daily necessity. The woods and forests higher up in the hills were full of life – prisoners, refugees and partisans, all being helped by the peasants.

A stranger, on whose youthful face a luxuriant black beard struck an incongruous note, came seeking Betty one morning. His hair too was long but his hirsute appearance was evidently intentional, for he was sleek and clean with long artistic hands.

Bowing low, he introduced himself: 'I am Count P., Signora. It is indeed miraculous to find so beautiful a lady in such lowly surroundings.'

Betty smiled faintly. She knew he had not come to this miserable village on a social call, so she waited patiently until the compliments were over and they could get down to business.

'Signora,' he said at last, 'I have come to make a suggestion about the British prisoners who are here.'

'Oh, are there British prisoners here?' Betty asked innocently.

Ignoring this, Count P. went on: 'We all feel they would be much safer in the mountains above Norcia, where there are well organised partisan bands. I myself could lead them from here across the German-occupied plains and up into the mountains. I know all the paths. Or I could send Captain Fiorani, who has already led many men up to the partisans.'

'Where do I fit into all this?' Betty asked.

Count P. looked grave. 'I want you to speak to the prisoners and try to persuade them to come with me, for their presence here is a constant menace for these little villages. The Germans know there are many English in these woods. Sooner or later there will be a raid and they will get caught. They would be much safer higher up in the mountains.'

Though she had not disclosed the fact, Betty knew of Count P., by name and reputation, but how was she to be certain that the man before her really was Count P., that he sincerely intended to lead the men to safety and was not going to hand them over to the Germans?

She answered vaguely. 'If by any chance I do see any prisoners, I'll mention it to them, but there aren't any around at the moment.'

Count P. looked at her slyly and almost winked. 'I know you don't trust me, but you are making a great mistake. You needn't commit yourself about the prisoners – I'm looking after several myself at my house above the next village – but you would be doing us and them a good turn if you could persuade them to come with me.'

Betty said she would see what she could do.

'It has been a great pleasure to talk with a lady as discreet and intelligent as she is lovely.' Count P. bowed once more and left.

The person to consult, Betty felt sure, was her friend the Sergeant-Major, but no one seemed to know where he was. Eventually, the know-all Giuseppe said he'd heard the tall Englishman was at San Severo and Betty tracked him down there visiting the Yorkshire lad, George, and McFee, his protector. She told him about Count P.'s visit and her misgivings and the Sergeant-Major asked her to describe him.

'That sounds like Count P. all right,' Michael said. 'He and Captain Fiorani have done some useful work. I know of several groups of prisoners whom they've led into the mountains to join Melis and his band.'

'Who exactly is Melis?' Betty asked. She had often heard the peasants speak of him with bated breath.

'Your husband may well know him,' St. John answered, 'because not only was he a regular Army officer, but he lived in Spoleto. After the German occupation he escaped from his regiment and made his way home with false papers. There he gathered some adventurous spirits around him and they went off into the mountains, forming the nucleus of what later became a very large band. Because of course they were soon joined by lots of young men trying to evade military service.'

'How do so many of them manage for food?'

'They levy toll on the peasants who originally fed and hid them.'

'Are they genuine partisans, would you say?'

'Well, they've been responsible for quite a bit of sabotage, so I'm told, blocking roads and blowing up bridges. Nothing very spectacular, it's true, but then they had no arms or equipment of any sort to start with. Later they raided dumps and got what they wanted. They even claim to have been supplied by parachute by the R.A.F. The Germans haven't mounted any large-scale operation against them yet, though they've taken reprisals against some wretched peasants who had nothing to do with the partisans. But there's no doubt about their nuisance value, anyway.'

Melis became a legendary hero in the coutryside and was invested with all the glamour of such figures. Tales were told of the valiant and daring feats he had performed, but a few weeks later he was captured as he lay very ill in a hut near Norcia. Fortunately, the Germans never discovered his true identity, but he was held 'on suspicion' and found himself ignominiously in prison. His band, however, continued.

Betty would have liked Michael St. John to have told her own prisoner friends about Count P.'s proposal, but the Sergeant-Major had promised to visit some other prisoners near a village some miles away, so she went herself to the derelict hut above the river. They were not enthusiastic.

'Some of our friends have been caught that way,' Fred said with a frown. 'I wouldn't trust nobody.'

'Ah would'nae join any band led by a bloody Itie – not after what I saw in the desert,' Fergus said. Then, remembering that Betty's husband was an Italian officer, he added hastily, 'though I dare say their regular army is a different matter.'

Count P. may have heard through the ubiquitous grapevine that Betty's recruiting campaign on his behalf had been a failure. At any rate she never saw him again.

'Why does he call himself Count P.?' Betty asked Michael St. John when she next met him. 'What's his real name?'

'A very illustrious one, I believe, one that goes right back to medieval days and that every educated Italian knows. He thinks that if the Germans or fascists knew it they would persecute other members of his family who have nothing to do with the partisans.'

Understandably, after so many months of prison, hearts were extremely susceptible and nearly all the prisoners were displaying varying symptoms of the love disease, some in the depths of despondency because they had nothing to offer for marriage and saw no future for themselves, others in the heights of ecstasy because some strapping peasant girl had bestowed a smile. In fact, some of the local girls were very attractive, Betty had to admit, and each day brought a succession of men to Piera's house with requests for an interpreter. Both she and the boys spent a lot of their time translating love letters for bashful girls, wondrous efforts with phonetic spelling and no punctuation, but expressing the most flowery thoughts, or else composing for the men on the theme 'till death us do part' or 'never really loved before'.

Betty was often asked to act as a kind of buffer between the parents and the lovers, or to engage them in conversation and find out which way the wind was blowing. Alec and Billy were roped in as Cupid's messengers to deliver the missive and report its effect on the recipient. 'Did she look pleased?' 'Did she blush?'

One day Alf appeared at the bottom of the steps with a sheepish grin on his face.

'I say, Betty, do you think you could do something for me? It's that there girl Liliana up at yon farm.' He waved vaguely in the direction of the hillside. 'She's a smashing kid and we have lots of jokes together, but as soon as I try to get her on to something serious she looks at me as though I was a blasted fascist and I can get nothing out of her. I want to marry her. I'll come back after the war, I swear I will – if I get through all right – and take up farming here. Will you ask her if she'll wait for me?'

'I've never proposed to anyone in my life,' Betty blurted out, taken aback by the prospect of doing so.

'No, of course not,' said Alf, shocked. 'But you'd only be doing it as a favour for a friend, like, wouldn't you?'

'It's a big responsibility.' Nor did it seem much of a bargain for Liliana, who knew nothing of Alf, but Betty couldn't say no to the beseeching look in his eyes.

'She's down by the wood by herself,' he said excitedly. 'If we go now, you can get her alone.'

So they walked down the fields until they discerned Liliana looking after a cow. Alf hid behind a hedge while Betty went across to the girl, who stood and watched her coming with resentful eyes under a mop of sun-bleached hair. Betty realised she wasn't a girl with whom one could dally in light conversation. The look in her eye said plainly 'State your business and go', so she came straight to the point.

'I believe you know an English prisoner called Alf?' Liliana nodded.

'He is a splendid young man and a great friend of mine. He has an excellent character and would make any girl an ideal husband, but he is most fastidious about women. When a young man like that falls in love he is quite serious and thinks only of marriage.'

Disappointingly for Betty, the magic word marriage produced not the slightest change in Liliana's sullen expression.

She struggled on. 'In his own country he has a good position' – Alf had told her he was a mechanic, living in Derby with his widowed mother – 'and a little house of his own, but he is quite willing to give all this up and return to Italy after the war if the girl of his choice prefers it. Now, Liliana, he has already made his choice, and I think you can guess who it is.'

The girl was looking at her as if she were an old boot, and poor Betty felt she was getting nowhere.

'It is you he loves and he wants to marry you. He will be true to you and he asks you to wait for him. After the war he will return – I'm quite certain of this – and if you love him too I know he could make you happy one day. What do you say?'

Liliana scratched herself thoughtfully and gave the cow a slap before answering.

'How can I be sure he'll return? I'll give him my answer when he comes back.'

'Don't you love him?'

'I'll tell him that too when he comes back.'

'Will you agree to wait for him?'

'No, but if I'm still free when he comes back, I'll consider it.'

There was nothing to be done against this native horse-sense.

Liliana was right, of course, and living as she did, close to the essentials of life, any fanciful ideas of love had no place in her make-up. Betty felt that against this instinctive wisdom it was no use persisting. But glancing over her shoulder she saw Alf's anxious face peering through the hedge, so she made a last effort.

'Can't you change your mind? He loves you so much. He needs you and you would make him so happy if you'd become engaged.'

But she repeated, with the same stolid indifference: 'If he comes back –' and Betty went away, a rejected proxy lover.

Poor Alf was desperately unhappy, but Betty felt sure that as soon as he returned to England the image of tow-headed Liliana would fade quickly from his mind.

The approaching winter and their primitive way of life made it almost inevitable that one or other of the family should catch cold. The wind howled through the loft and there was no way of keeping it out. It whistled through the crevices between the stones and around the newspapers with which they had surrounded the window.

This window was a show-piece. It was brand new, with shining panes of glass mounted in a frame of freshly painted wood, but the whole thing had been lightheartedly pushed into the hole in the wall left for a window and then just abandoned. No attempt had been made to fill up the ragged gaps between the frame and the wall or to fix it in any way, and they were always expecting the whole thing to fall out at the slightest breeze. There were no nails, nor any other visible means of attachment, yet there it firmly stayed in its aperture, through hail and blizzard, for the whole of their stay, fixed in position presumably by faith.

When it rained the roof dripped impartially on beds and clothes, and they moved according to the drips. The loft would often present a strangely confused appearance, with all the beds at different angles here and there in the room, as though the family had been quarrelling violently.

The food was filling enough but contained very little nourishment beyond vitamins. Hitherto no one had been ill, but one day Teresa ran a temperature. Luckily it was fine and the loft was dry so she stayed in bed.

Michael St. John, who had been a medical student, came and looked at her. 'I agree with you,' he told her mother, 'I think she's got tonsilitis.' So Betty started a campaign of linseed plasters and vinegar gargles.

At lunch time Piera told her: 'The priest at San Severo is a bit of a doctor. He's often called in for sick people.'

That afternoon Betty sent Enrico over there to ask him to come. In a very short time he arrived, striding like a fury along the road and leaving clouds of dust stirred up by his voluminous black skirts, with Enrico panting along behind trying to keep up. A tall gaunt man he was, untidy and dirty, and Betty remembered him at Sabatino's funeral, fuming in the road beside the coffin.

This black, fierce-looking figure craning over her bedside frightened Teresa, who howled, but he gradually won her over and confirmed their diagnosis.

'You must get some medicine. Can someone go down to Spoleto for it?'

Enrico had never been to the town during their stay at Roselli and was longing to go and see his friends. As Betty's fears of the fascists had been somewhat lulled since her encounter with the deserters, she arranged that Agnese should take him down in her trap and he was soon off.

There was another reason why one of them should go to Spoleto as both Roselli and the nearest village, San Severo, were out of salt and could get no new supplies. To lack salt in cooking is a disaster. After a time it is almost impossible to eat, even if one is hungry. The food tastes nauseating and the craving for salt becomes an obsession. Though most of the peasants still had some in their houses Betty didn't like to take theirs because of the shortage, so she had told Enrico he must ask Giulia to procure some for them. Meanwhile, she sat down beside Teresa's bed.

In due course Enrico arrived at Spoleto. Leaving Agnese to do her own jobs, he took the short-cut past the hospital to Casa San Marzano. He found Giulia at work in the stables, but as soon as she heard that medicines were needed for Teresa, she cleaned herself up and set off at once for the town. While she was gone, Enrico took the opportunity to visit two of his school friends and hear the latest news, which didn't seem to be very exciting.

In an hour Giulia returned with the medicines and also some black market salt, and Enrico, stuffing his knapsack full with some clothes which he needed, ran down through the fields to wait for Agnese. He climbed the bank which led to the path round the back of the hospital and, pushing through the hedge, found himself face to face with two fascist militiamen. Too late he started to scramble back.

'Hey! Stop! Come here. What are you doing?'

'Nothing.'

'What do you mean, "nothing"?'

'I'm waiting for a cart to San Giovanni.'

'What's in that knapsack?'

'Clothes.'

'Let's see.'

They opened the knapsack and spread everything out on the ground: the medicines, the black market salt, the clothes and all the little treasures that Enrico had collected in the house; a small book of English songs; and a notebook in which he used to jot down the times of the B.B.C. broadcasts in Italian from London and also the wavelengths of several foreign stations which they always listened to because they gave a truer picture of the progress of the war than did the fascist-controlled programmes.

Of course it was forbidden on pain of death to listen to foreign broadcasts and Enrico's blood ran cold as the two militiamen started examining the rows of figures. These they looked at very carefully for several minutes, thrilled to have found something really suspicious, while Enrico stood by in agony, wondering whether it would be better to make a dash for it or try to brazen it out. The men were big, and armed, so he decided against an escape bid.

'You'll have to explain this to the Captain. Come with us.'

Having stuffed everything back into the knapsack, they started off, one on each side of Enrico, down the covered way which led to the hospital, through the Porta Loreto and up to the fascist militia barracks. On the way they passed another school friend of Enrico's and his startled face heightened the boy's misery.

On arrival he was pushed into a whitewashed room where he sat dejectedly, gazing at the wall on which the fascist slogan '*Credere, Obbedire, Combattere*' was painted under a crude stencil portrait of Mussolini. In one corner was a pile of rifles and shotguns, but no ammunition. Through the window he could see the roofs of Spoleto with lines of washing dancing gaily in the sunshine.

He examined the room, but it offered no chance of escape. The single window had a bar down the middle, leaving spaces too small to squeeze through. Moreover, it gave on to the front of the barracks and occasionally Enrico could see the cap of the sentry below, as his pacing brought him into view.

Enrico had his head pressed against the bar of the window when the guard came to escort him to the Captain's office to be questioned. Behind the desk sat a small dark man with bristly hair, writing, but he motioned to the guard to leave him alone with the boy and, laying down his pen, picked up the incriminating notebook.

'Is this yours?'

'Yes, sir.'

'Where do you come from?'

'San Giovanni.'

'What is your name?'

'Enrico di San Marzano.'

The man wrote it down, then paused as a thought struck him.

'There was a Major of that name commanding a battalion of the

Cacciatori Regiment here, some years before the war. Any relation?'

'Yes, sir, my father.'

The small man beamed. 'Ah. He was a friend of mine. We had many interesting talks together. Where is he now?'

'He's with the Army, up north.'

'Is he fighting with the fascist army?'

'Oh yes, sir,' Enrico lied brightly, though he knew well that his father was almost certainly a fugitive, helping to organise partisan resistance.

'That's splendid. Give him my regards when you write. Don't know why these fools of soldiers brought you in. They should have known who you were. One gets a poor type of recruit these days. By the way, what are those rows of figures in your notebook that made my men so suspicious?'

'They are the wavelengths of various German stations.'

Enrico hoped the Captain hadn't much time for listening to the radio, as it would be obvious to anyone who did that the numbers were not those of Italian or German stations.

'Oh, that's all right, then. Here's your book. You can go, but be sure to remember me to your father.'

With a spectacular fascist salute Enrico withdrew. He shot out of the barracks, forced himself to walk slowly until he was out of sight round a corner, then took to his heels and ran as long as his breath lasted, putting as much distance as possible between himself and the Captain, lest the latter should find out that the San Marzanos were wanted by the fascist police. Luckily there was some rivalry between the police and the militia, and they often spoilt each other's ploys by petty jealousy and squabbles.

Despite his hair-raising adventure, Enrico was in time to catch Agnese, who had been delayed. He arrived back at Roselli with the salt and medicines intact and, more important, himself.

The medicines that Enrico had nearly forfeited his freedom to obtain did the trick, and Teresa was only in bed for a few days, but Betty vowed never to let her oldest son out of her sight again.

Since Sabatino's death there had been no one to collect firewood.

'Why don't we get our own?' Alec suggested. 'I know where there's a dead tree.'

They set off, armed with axes and choppers and accompanied by two Canadian prisoners who had recently arrived at Roselli, Lloyd and Len. Lloyd had been a lumberman and Len claimed membership of the North-West Mounted Police, so they seemed to be the most expert on matters of timber.

As the morning wore on the log pile grew, and it was about five feet high in the middle of a clearing when they heard the sound of an aircraft approaching.

Peering up through the branches as the machine came overhead, Len said: 'It's an old Jerry Stork. I know they had one on Foligno airfield, and I suppose that's it.'

'What do they use if for?' Betty asked.

'It's an observation plane,' Lloyd said shortly.

By mid-day they had collected a tremendous amount of wood, and they spent the afternoon dragging it down to the village with the aid of several more prisoners. That evening the stable was piled high with firewood and faggots, to Piera's great joy, and even the gaunt pig seemed pleased to have a change of scenery.

Every day after this the German Stork would chug over the tree-tops, like an airborne sewing machine, apparently trying to locate prisoners in the woods. The men would laugh derisively as it passed over, but those still in uniform would take cover. Whether the subsequent events were a result of these flights they never knew.

As time went on Piera's attitude became increasingly distant and unhelpful. She resented the presence of an English family, not because she disliked them personally but because of the danger they represented to her household. She had forbidden any prisoner to set foot in the house, though she would send out food if anyone was in need.

'It's Domenico, the surly brute,' Enrico said. 'He's put the wind up her.'

Betty felt they could not stay there much longer, though where else to go presented a major problem. She decided to go down to Spoleto to glean a little news, to see Angelina and consult her as to whether it would be wiser to remain at Roselli, return to the town or look for another hiding place.

Favi, the prosperous farmer who had given a home to Caterina, offered to take her in his trap and they set off in the pale dawn. The open trap was very cold. Betty now owned no stockings, the raw air turned her legs blue and her feet ached agonisingly throughout the journey. The normally jovial Favi was taciturn, apparently absorbed in his own affairs. Betty was not sorry to be left to hers, although her thoughts centred mainly on her toes, wondering whether they were still there. She managed to jump off at the hospital, however, Favi promising to pick her up there at two o'clock. When she had thawed her feet a little by stamping on them, she ran up to Angelina's house.

It was good to see her friend again, to be welcomed so warmly, to expand in a comfortable home and drink wine out of a proper wine glass. They exchanged news and talked for some time about their children. Then, as she had to prepare a meal, Angelina took Betty with her into the large kitchen, its rows of shining copper pans somewhat depleted since the fascists had 'requisitioned' quite a lot of them.

Watching Angelina knead the dough for the *pasta*, Betty broached the subject of returning to her house.

Angelina's face clouded. 'I really don't know how to advise you. I have been putting off talking to you about it, but I think I ought to warn you there's a well-founded rumour that the Germans are going to occupy your house, as it is standing empty, and use it for officers' billets.'

'Oh Lord!' Betty gasped, her worst fears confirmed.

'Also I know that the fascists have found out where you are hiding and they believe – though they have no proof – that you are helping escaped prisoners. Therefore it would be wiser for you to move and hide again.'

Hide again? Still hunted? The whole world seemed to be reeling round her and gradually receding, leaving her without substance. No home – nothing left – nowhere to go. As long as she had the house Betty felt subconsciously that they were not totally without a base, but if the house were taken away, where could they go? If the fascists were on their trail they could not stay in Roselli. Besides, she had no money left at all. She had paid Piera and Beppe, the miller, and bought vegetables, apples, eggs and milk.

So what was she to do? If it had not been for Billy and Teresa she would have joined the men going south, or tried with the older boys to get through to the Allied lines. But the smaller children made this impossible. Their short legs could not carry them over the mountains, with the winter setting in and snow already on the peaks and passes. Who would help or shelter them? Who was altruistic or foolhardy enough to take on the responsibility of an English family?

The world indeed seemed hopeless as Betty sat before the stove, gazing into the burning embers, and the black bars, symbolic against the glowing fire, brought to life the dread, ever present at the back of her mind, of a concentration camp and all its obscenity.

Betty looked at Angelina. There she sat at the table, comely in her blue overall, arms buried in the flour, dark compassionate eyes watching her across the room. Poor Angelina, she had so many difficulties of her own that Betty knew she must not burden her with her own dismay.

'Oh well, we'll be all right, I expect,' she said, getting up and trying to keep the hopelessness out of her voice. 'Thank you for warning me. I'll return to Roselli now and think things over. Somehow or other I'll let you know where we go and what we do.'

It was not yet time for Favi to pick her up, but she was too agitated to remain in her own house. She made her way back to the hospital and paced up and down in the road until she heard the pony trap rattling round the corner.

Betty clambered in and gave herself over to despairing thoughts until the insistent pressure of her companion's arm and knee on her own alerted her to the fact that he was a great deal closer than the shortness of the seat necessitated. She edged away until she was half hanging over the road, whereupon a stalwart arm encircled her waist and hoisted her back.

'I know I'm a lucky man to have such a pretty girl for a passenger,' Favi said, 'but you wouldn't deny me a kiss, now, would you?'

'This is the last straw!' Betty thought, as her face was brushed by a bristly stubble and a strong aroma of wine enveloped her. She gave him a mighty shove, which almost toppled him from his perch and made him clutch at the reins, bringing the pony to an abrupt halt. Then, seeing his hurt, startled and guilty look, her sense of humour came to her rescue and she burst out laughing.

Surprised and delighted to be forgiven, Favi's ruddy features broke into a smile and Betty gave him a chaste kiss on the cheek to show she was not offended. He became lively and amusing and Betty even felt grateful to him for chasing away her black forebodings.

'You're in a much better mood than you were this morning,' she pointed out. 'What's made you so cheerful?'

'I did a fair deal in the town, and I had a glass or two to celebrate it.'

'You didn't have to tell me that,' she said with a grin.

That night, however, depression and anxiety returned. Sleep was out of the question, but as the hours of darkness dragged slowly by she could think of no solution to their problem. Next morning, tired and worried, she was snappy with the children and had to remind herself that her dilemma was no fault of theirs.

After breakfast Antonio came in to tell Betty that a man from Spoleto had arrived in a pony trap and was asking for her.

'Oh my God,' she thought, 'they've tracked us down already.'

But the boy, seeing her alarmed look, hastily added, 'He's not a fascist.' So they walked down the street to see who it was.

He was short and rotund, with bow legs, hairless eyebrows and very fair eyelashes which gave his face a blank and slightly startled expression. They shook hands and he introduced himself as Sabatino Sabatini.

'Signora,' he said, 'I know your husband well. I am a Maresciallo (Sergeant-Major) in the 52nd Regiment of Cacciatori delle Alpi and served under the Colonello here for some time. This has given me the courage to come and ask a favour of you.'

'I'm afraid I am hardly in a position to grant favours to anyone, however much I might want to,' Betty replied with a wry smile.

'In my case, however, I believe you are, Signora,' he persisted. 'Let me explain. I live with my wife in a little house near the station in Spoleto. My wife is a nervy woman and she is terrified by the bombing. I shall have no peace until I find a place for us in the country. She cries night and day and the children howl in sympathy. I would do anything to get them all away from the town. I know you have a villa up in the hills above Spoleto. As soon as I heard you were away and the house empty, I made every effort to trace you so as to come and ask you if we could rent your house. Now I have found you –'

Betty interrupted him. 'Is it so easy to trace us, then? I came here secretly, believing no one would know, but you seem to have found me.'

'Ah, Signora, it was not easy, but many people know your whereabouts all the same.'

This staggered her.

'But it doesn't matter,' he went on. 'Cesarino Matafia, your worst enemy, fled yesterday, also Bartozzini and several of the other fanatical fascists.'

'What made them go?'

'They think the Allies will be here soon and they'd better escape while the going is good and establish themselves up north. Spoleto is cleaned up. The worst fascist element is gone – disappeared overnight – and the ones that are left have no grudge against you. Would you be willing to rent me your house?'

Betty could hardly believe her ears. Here was the solution to her problem. With the house occupied by someone in an official position – for he would still be in the Army – it was much less likely to be requisitioned by the Germans, and with her special enemies out of the way the fascists seemed less of a menace. Though he didn't look much like a heavenly messenger, Betty could have embraced the Maresciallo.

'Of course,' she said, 'and willingly. But I couldn't let you have the whole house.'

'We would be content with a room or two and the use of the kitchen as long as we were away from the bombs.'

And so it was concluded, the price fixed and everything settled. Pulling a wad of notes from his pocket, the Maresciallo handed Betty the first month's rent and she felt they were rich indeed. They went along to Piera's house to see if they could beg a half-litre of wine to celebrate and she, sensing that change was in the air and that they might be leaving, produced not only wine but bread and ham too.

With a man in Casa San Marzano Betty felt that perhaps they could return home. She told Piera they would probably be going and her face lost some of its habitually worried expression.

'We'll probably be safer there than here,' Enrico said. 'Why don't we go tomorrow, Mummy?'

There was a chorus of assent from the other children. The thought of being in their own home again was so overwhelmingly attractive that Betty quickly agreed.

'I'll go and find a cart to carry our things,' Alec said.

'I don't think we'll bother about the beds,' Betty said. 'We'll be less conspicuous with just our hand luggage.'

Piera happily agreed that the beds could be stacked in a corner of the loft.

Teresa suddenly piped up excitedly: 'Mummy! Mummy! We'll be able to have Caterina back.'

In truth Betty had forgotten about the little donkey. 'I hope so, darling,' she answered rather doubtfully, 'provided Favi's children haven't become too fond of her.'

'The peasants don't make pets of horses and donkeys, like we do,' Enrico pointed out. 'I expect they've been using her to collect firewood and things like that.'

'Oh please, Mummy,' Teresa begged, 'let's go over there and get her back.'

'There are some prisoners living at Pian della Noce, aren't there, Mum?' Alec asked.

'Yes, we ought to say goodbye to them.'

'Come on then!' Teresa raced off ahead of them.

Favi was as good-natured about letting the donkey go as he had been about taking her in, and his children didn't seem unduly upset at Teresa's resuming possession of her beloved pet.

Favi, on his best behaviour, introduced them to his family and also to several youths who seemed to have no particular abode or means of livelihood. These were typical of the thousands of young men hiding in the mountains to escape military service, just existing where and as best they could, while their families in the town smuggled them food.

Sometimes, when the men did not answer the call-up, the fascist authorities blackmailed the families by removing all their ration books, so that very often, to prevent their families from dying of starvation, the men would be forced to give themselves up. But others managed to live on stolen or black-market food, and on occasions the tables were turned and the young men scrounged food from outlying farms and smuggled it back into town for their families.

They started their homeward walk at twilight, with Teresa leading Caterina. At Santino's farm they stopped to say goodbye to the two Reggies, who had sought refuge there after their cave had become too cold and damp to be habitable. Santino had thought up a cunning hiding place for them. In the side of the haystack facing the woods he had cut a small hole at ground level, about a foot square, and a small passage leading right into the heart of the stack where he had hollowed out just enough space for the two of them. No one could spot the entrance as it was covered by overhanging wisps of hay. The children were delighted with this warm and cosy cubby-hole, which they crawled into and out of, one after the other.

'I wish *we* could spend the night there, Mummy,' Billy said.

The two Reggies joined them and they sauntered back towards Roselli, enjoying the beautiful afterglow of the sunset and the soft peace that seemed to steal over everything. They looked up at the black woods above them, so still and silent, yet they knew that beneath those trees was life, that all sorts of activities were going on there and schemes, good and bad, were being hatched.

While they watched, a light flickered in the trees far up the mountainside. Long-short, long-short, it flashed. The boys could all read a little Morse, but could make no sense of the signals.

'Probably some code,' Enrico said.

'Is it the fascists, do you think?' Reggie, the butcher, asked.

'Very unlikely,' Betty answered. 'They seldom dare venture into the hills at night.'

With desperate men lurking in the black woods, a dagger thrust in the dark was the least to be expected.

'Probably partisans,' Alec said. 'I wish we knew what the message was, what plans they are making.'

They set off down the long field above the village when below them, by the hedge, an enormous figure loomed up, standing motionless awaiting their approach. As they drew nearer Betty recognised Michael St. John, with Alf and the fair-haired Jack, whom Teresa would normally have run to greet.

But there was something in the waiting men's attitude that chilled them, and as Betty came up to them she could see, even in the half-darkness, that Michael looked tense and different from his usual assured self.

'What's happened?' she asked.

'They've been beating us up.'

'Who?'

'The fascists. This afternoon I was in my room at Angelo's farm when I heard voices. Looking through the window I saw several fascists with sub-machine-guns asking for Giovanni.'

Giovanni was Angelo's sixteen-year-old son.

'He was in the farmyard, but when he realised they were searching for him he ran out of the gate and started dashing across the field. They called to him but the silly boy wouldn't stop, so one of them shot him down with his *mitra*. They all had *mitras*, so I didn't wait to hear any more but jumped from the loft to the other side of the farmhouse. Then I ran to warn Jack and Alf, who had gone to visit another farm.'

'Lucky you did,' Jack said, putting an arm round Teresa.

'After they had shot the boy,' Michael went on, 'they all became very excited and scattered, shouting and searching. They fired at me, but I ran behind some trees and they didn't bother to follow. I don't think they can have seen me properly or they'd have spotted my khaki.'

Alf took up the story. 'I hid behind a hedge to watch what happened. The bastards went off towards Spoleto eventually.'

'They probably want to get clear of the forest before dark,' Michael said.

'It looks as if we have till tomorrow morning, then,' Betty said, making an effort to speak casually.

Michael nodded. 'I don't think it's a proper comb-out yet. I saw Baldino with the fascists. I think they're just nosing out the prisoners' hiding places. When they know a bit more they'll bring up the Germans.'

Baldino was the village fascist. He worked in Spoleto as a sergeant in the militia, and therefore only came to Roselli occasionally, but his approach was always heralded so that on his arrival in the village no khaki figures were ever about and all was quiet and peaceful. But he evidently knew of the prisoners' presence in the neighbourhood and had brought up some fascists today to question Giovanni's father. The boy died almost immediately after the shooting, but they all knew that this was the prelude to something even worse.

'What are you going to do?' Betty asked Michael.

'I think tomorrow we'd better set off south. Luckily, I managed to grab most of my kit before I left, and Alf and Jack have theirs.'

'What about Fergus and the other lads in the log cabin?'

Alf answered. 'They decided to beat it directly after the shooting. Hamish said he wasn't going to wait for Jerry to come and collect him. They sent lots of messages to you and the children, Betty. They were real sorry not to have said goodbye.'

'I'm sorry too,' Betty said. She had come to regard the stalwart Scotsmen as a solid rock on which the prisoner community round Roselli was founded. Their precipitate departure brought home to her the full extent of the crisis they were facing even more than the tragic shooting of the poor boy, whom she had known only by sight.

Michael turned to the two Reggies. 'Will you warn the others at Pian della Noce while I go off to San Severo and tell the men there? Giovanni's brother has gone to Case Nuove to give the alarm, and the rumour of a round-up will soon spread, but I think the bands further up the mountains are quite safe. The Germans won't bother to send much of a force up here for a few harmless prisoners. They'll probably send the fascists, so it will be just these first few villages that will be hit.'

'What about tonight?'

'Oh, we'll go somewhere up in the woods. Luckily, we've got our greatcoats.'

But Enrico piped up: 'I say, I know a wonderful place. Alec and I discovered it one day. It's a deserted broken-down cottage in a ravine above the village, quite hidden in the trees with a stream running past the door. We built a dam across the water – I bet it's still there – but it's a super place to hide.'

'Sounds O.K.,' Michael said. 'No one will be coming up till tomorrow so we might as well sleep there tonight. Lead on, young man.'

They thought they would all go and take a look at the place. The men skirted the village while Betty and the children ran to Piera's house, put Caterina in the stable, took three blankets from their beds and some bread and cheese, and joined the men on the road past Roselli. Alec had brought half a candle and some matches. It was the last candle they had and they had been dressing in the dark for some days now, keeping the candle for just such an emergency as had now arisen.

They set off down the ravine, scrambling amongst the rocks and bushes. There was a moon so they could see fairly well, though it was dark under the trees. As the boys led them further down into the valley they saw the outline of the tumbledown place before them, looking most romantic in the moonlight.

Inside they picked out what they could by the glimmer of the candle, peering into the bare rooms where spiders' webs formed curtains across the rafters and brushed their faces like ghostly hands pushing back the intruders, and rats scurried away.

It was certainly an ideal place for playing robbers, for it had something fairy-tale about it, as if the genie of the place would presently appear and transform it into Ali Baba's cave. It stood alone in the moonlight surrounded by tall trees, with the dam that the boys had built just by the door where the water had trickled over, leaving a muddy patch on the path. But they were not there to play pirates or robbers, and the thought that this dream-like place was the scene of a real game of life or death thrilled the children, particularly Enrico and Alec, who had discovered it in the first place and could now feel that they were actively helping three British prisoners. Meanwhile, Billy and Teresa ran excitedly from room to room, finding some little sweet apples in one place and some straw in another.

The men threw their blankets and packs on the straw and Alf lay down, no doubt to dream of Liliana.

'I must warn the boys at San Severo before I turn in,' Michael said, stifling a yawn. 'I'll take a short cut through the woods.'

'Will you find your way back all right?' Enrico asked.

'Oh yes, I'm used to travelling by night and there's a good moon.'

'I'll come with you,' said Jack.

'So will I,' said Teresa, taking Jack's hand. She hated the idea of having to say goodbye to him again after his miraculous return.

'If we go to San Severo we'd better take the road,' Betty said.

They had a lot of friends there whom they wanted to say goodbye to: Signora Sinibaldi, whose son, a school-friend of Enrico's, helped the peasants to carry a cauldron of soup a couple of miles up the mountain every day for the prisoners hiding there; the priest; George, now nearly well, McFee and several other prisoners lodging in various houses.

When they arrived they found half a dozen of them sitting in the wine shop. Michael had evidently not got as far as that yet, and Betty was reluctant to spoil their cheerfulness, but presently Jack appeared and gave them the bad news.

Later they found Michael at the priest's house, where he had gone to seek a blessing before setting forth next morning. Then they walked back together towards Roselli, saying goodbye at the top of the ravine.

It was a sad moment, for in this time of stress they had come to feel very close to the prisoners. Would they ever see each other again?

'See you after the war, I promise, sweetie,' Jack was murmuring to a tearful Teresa.

'We'll meet in London,' Michael assured Betty as they turned up the village street.

But London seemed part of another existence, and would the war ever end?

During what was left of the night they packed and got ready their things, while Billy and Teresa slept peacefully. Next morning they left in two donkey carts, one of them pulled by the faithful Caterina.

Betty did not want to be found if the Germans or the fascists raided the village. Too much seemed to be known of her activities with the P.O.W.s and it now looked safer for them in Spoleto, where she could deny all knowledge of the prisoners of Roselli.

As they reached the bottom of the hill they took a last look at the little village. That part of their lives was over and in a few hours' time they would begin something new, but behind them they were leaving good friends and the memory of those months of comradeship meant much to them.

Turning, Betty saw Michael beside the road. He had cut down through the fields to bid them a last farewell.

'Some of us have already left this morning and more are going in a few minutes. I'm off this afternoon. Soon the village will be deserted by us all. Others will come, I expect, but we shall have gone our different ways.'

So saying, he saluted and, turning, walked back into the woods.

PART III
Paying and Non-Paying Guests

The two carts creaked slowly up the steep dust road from Spoleto and the exhausted donkeys turned the last bend, bringing the gates of Casa San Marzano into view. Ever since their precipitate flight after the Italian Armistice the harsh repression of the German occupation had been steadily increasing, together with the militancy of the local fascists, until the sudden and unexpected flight of their leaders a day or two ago, and Betty had abandoned hope of seeing her home again. The sight of it now brought tears to her eyes and a ragged cheer from her tired but happy children.

A small figure was playing with a ball a few yards from their gates.

'Clelia!' shouted Teresa, jumping down from the first donkey cart and rushing up the track. Her little friend turned, eyes and mouth wide open in amazement, and Teresa stopped dead, overcome by shyness after their long separation. A moment later they were gabbling away happily in Italian and, hearing their voices, the faithful Giulia ran out to greet them all.

'Oh, Signora, what a wonderful surprise!' She reached up to help Betty down from the cart. 'We've been so worried about you.'

Betty embraced her fondly. 'Now I know I really am home. Have Maresciallo Sabatini and his family shown up yet? I've let them some rooms.'

'Yes, they moved in yesterday.'

'How many are there in the family?'

'Well, there's the Maresciallo himself – he'll be at work at the Army depot in Spoleto now, of course – Signora Sabatini – I've heard him call her Olga – his sister Eugenia, and their two little girls – Graziella, she's the eldest, about eight I should say, and Fiorella – she told Clelia she was six.'

'That makes five, then. We shall be a bit crowded, shan't we, Giulia?' But Betty was so pleased to be home again that she didn't really care.

At that point Olga Sabatini, accompanied by her sister-in-law Eugenia, came out into the courtyard to welcome them.

'We're so very grateful to you, Contessa, for allowing us to live in your house,' Olga said. 'The bombing was terrible. Really terrible! I couldn't have stood it a day longer. I should have gone mad.'

Betty could see the signs of strain on her sensitive, intelligent face. By contrast Eugenia looked to be of stolid peasant stock. 'I wouldn't be surprised if that one slept through the air raids,' Betty thought to herself.

The two older boys were hastily unloading the donkey carts, Enrico eager to go and look up old friends and Alec to fuss over his precious rabbits. Billy had gone off to unearth some of the toys he had had to leave behind, and Teresa had been taken by Clelia to meet Graziella and Fiorella Sabatini.

Able to relax at last, Betty realised that she was physically and mentally exhausted after the tension of the last two days. Taking leave of her tenants, she slipped away to the drawing room and sank gratefully into a deep armchair, a luxury she had almost forgotten.

Her peaceful reverie was short-lived. She heard the familiar clatter of wooden clogs and Serafina stormed into the room.

'Signora, have you seen the kitchen?'

'No, Serafina, what's the matter with it?'

'The matter with it? *Porca miseria*, it's in a terrible mess. Those women have strewn their stuff all over everywhere. They haven't left a square centimetre for us. And they've been using all our things and then putting them back in the wrong places. I can't find anything. The cupboards are full of their mugs and dishes all muddled up with ours. And that's not all . . .'

Serafina took a deep breath, but a button popped off her tight skirt, revealing another circle of plump flesh, and distracted her long enough for Betty to cut short her diatribe.

'Now look here, Serafina. Whom would you prefer to see living in this house? Us and the Sabatini family or the Germans?'

'But, Signora – '

'There are no "ifs" or "buts" about it. Maresciallo Sabatini is an N.C.O. in the Italian Army. With him and his family living here we have some chance of persuading the Germans not to requisition the house. Without them we have none. It's as simple as that.'

'But how can I look after you and cook for you, Signora, when those women have taken possession of my kitchen?'

'Part of the agreement that I made with the Maresciallo was that his family could share the use of the kitchen. How could the poor things cook their food otherwise?'

Serafina shrugged. Clearly to her this was a matter of little importance.

'Apart from all that,' Betty went on, 'the Maresciallo is paying me quite a reasonable rent. I have no other source of income, so without that money I probably wouldn't be able to buy anything for you to cook for us anyway.'

Unable to think of an answer to this, Serafina sighed deeply, thereby putting the rest of her skirt buttons in jeopardy.

'Ask Signora Sabatini to be kind enough to come and speak to me when she has a moment,' Betty told the maid. 'She seems sensible. I'm sure we can work something out.'

'Very well, Signora.' Serafina shook her head sadly and withdrew. A few minutes later there was a gentle knock on the door and Olga Sabatini entered. When Betty had explained Serafina's misgivings about sharing the kitchen, she looked very unhappy.

'I'm very sorry indeed to have upset your maid, Contessa,' she said. 'The fact is that we didn't expect you so soon. Otherwise I would have made sure everything was in order.'

Betty hastened to reassure her. 'Don't take too much notice of Serafina. She's liable to fly off the handle, but she's a good sort at heart and her fits of pique never last long. We've been used to sharing a kitchen at Roselli, where everything was pretty primitive, so it shouldn't be too difficult to work out a system here.'

Olga Sabatini proved to be a tactful as well as an intelligent woman, and she soon learned the right way to handle Serafina. So with goodwill and tolerance the two *ménages* managed to avoid friction.

A strange interim period ensued. In the south the front seemed to have been temporarily stabilised, and everyone was waiting for the next move. With the flight of the leading fascists from Spoleto, the Germans had virtually taken over the higher administration of the town, a change for the good as far as Betty and her family were concerned.

More disturbingly, however, they had established their Kommandatur at Villa Milani, the big house further up the hill which completely overlooked Casa San Marzano.

'It's rather nerve-wracking,' Betty said to Angelina de Marchis, who had come over to welcome them back. 'From up there they can watch every move we make, if they feel so inclined. However, we haven't been molested so far.'

'Alfonso was told the other day that their commanding officer is of Italian extraction and quite sympathetic to the population,' Angelina replied.

'All things considered, I think we really were in greater danger at Roselli after the fascist raid.'

The few German soldiers who strolled up the hill past the house in their free time seemed to be pleasant enough. In strict confidence they would tell Betty how much they were longing to be out of it all and back home with their families. Then out would come the inevitable photographs of wife and kids.

The main problems were still the same: how to make their money suffice; how to get enough to eat; and how to live in peace with their neighbours, for on small rations and beset with anxiety they were all easily upset or irritated.

About twice a week Betty would go into the town in the early morning to fetch their meagre rations. She could trust no one else to bring back the precious shopping. They were all so hungry that the bread would have been devoured before it ever reached the house.

In some ways they were even worse off than they had been at Roselli. Bread and pasta were now severely rationed, and there was no Beppe the miller to sell them extra flour. There was still no butter or milk, and cheese, meat and eggs were extremely scarce. The consignment of sugar came so irregularly that they did not know how to eke out their tiny ration. For a hot drink they toasted and ground acorns, which looked like coffee when percolated, but neither smelt nor tasted like it.

If the rations had been available regularly it would have been easier to manage, but they were in an occupied country and transport for the civilian population was chaotic, with no petrol except on the black market.

They were always hungry. The women especially suffered from running sores on legs and arms, certainly caused by deficiencies in the diet, especially as they invariably gave up their eggs, cheese and meat to the children who, strangely enough, always seemed to be bounding in vitality. Betty's used to swap fruit, which was still on the market, for a chunk of bread from the peasant children. Vegetable soup and salads still formed the staple diet, and though potatoes were scarce one could generally find a few. Even olive oil was rationed, but as Umbria is an olive-producing region there was not much difficulty in obtaining extra. There was, of course, a flourishing black market, but as they had no spare money they could not take advantage of it.

Betty never went into the town in the middle of the day, but they could get down to their friends the de Marchis by back ways, across the fields and behind the hospital.

School started, and each morning the gang of children, Betty's four, the Sabatini's and the peasant girls, streamed out of the house and rushed down the hill, to return at lunch-time with huge appetites which were difficult to satisfy.

It was getting colder and colder and promised a very severe winter. Keeping warm became a major problem. Casa San Marzano had wood-burning terracotta stoves in the living room and in Betty's bedroom, which they used as a study.

One afternoon after school Betty received a visit from one of the teachers, Professore Lombardo.

'By next week, Contessa,' he told her, 'we shall have burnt up all our fuel. As you know, I've asked all the children to bring overcoats or waterproofs to use as rugs in class, but some of them haven't got either.'

'I might be able to lend you a few old blankets.'

'I try to keep them on the move, with a run round the yard between classes as well as in the break, but so much exercise is not good for their concentration and the little ones get tired.'

'How would it be if each child brought a small log to help stoke the stoves?' Betty suggested.

The Professore scratched his bald head thoughtfully. 'It's an idea, Contessa, although the children who live in the town may have difficulty in finding any. But thank you, it's worth trying.'

Next morning the small children set off armed with a log each, while Enrico and Alec slung a sackful over their shoulders. As the temperature dropped, however, the supply of logs was consumed ever more quickly, and the school was eventually forced to close. The children were thus back on Betty's hands full time.

They made daily trips into the woods to collect firewood, but by December it was freezing and then the snow came down, burying the sticks on the ground and making them difficult to find.

The air raids started again, and some of the strained look re-appeared on Olga Sabatini's kindly face.

'But I feel much safer up here,' she assured Betty. 'I really am grateful to you for letting us live in your house.'

'I'm grateful to you for the rent,' Betty replied. 'Without it I don't know what I should do for money.'

Because of the bombing, the mothers preferred their children to keep out of the town all day, so schoolmates and friends plodded up the hill to the house, bringing their own little packets of lunch.

'I feel as if I was running a school,' Betty remarked to Olga, watching them as they dashed around in the snow to keep themselves warm.

Alec ran up to them. 'Can we get out the old toboggan, Mum?'

Soon a greatly overloaded toboggan was hurtling down the steep slope from just below Villa Milani to the vineyard of Casa San

Marzano, much to the amusement of the German soldiers at the Kommandatur, who looked as if they would have liked to join in.

When the snow thawed they played football or netball on the large space in front of the house, formerly the threshing ground, or dug an encampment surrounded by a palisade at the end of the garden. When it was wet they crowded round the stove, playing bingo or cards. In the evenings, when the gang of boys had returned to their homes, Betty would read aloud to her four, in English and Italian on alternate days. Sometimes they joined the Sabatinis in the kitchen.

On the advice of Alfonso de Marchis, Betty walled in her radio, with an unobstrusive switch in a corner. Thus she could tune in to the B.B.C.'s European Service from London, always preceded by the stirring first notes of Beethoven's Fifth Symphony.

With Christmas came a return of the snow and ice. Olga Sabatini, still fearful of air raids, had made one of her rare trips to Spoleto.

'There's absolutely nothing in the shops,' she reported with a long face. 'What are the children going to say? No presents for any of them, rich or poor.'

'I'm trying to make a rag doll for Teresa,' Betty said, 'but it looks as if the poor boys will just have to do without.'

Olga, with two little girls, jumped at the idea of rag dolls. 'Do you mind if I copy you, Signora?' she asked, and with Betty's amused consent started work on them straight away.

'At least we can have a Christmas tree,' Enrico pointed out when told of the empty shops.

They went up to the woods and cut down a magnificent one with plenty of greenery. It stood in the middle of the sitting room, with its top touching the beams, resplendent in tinsel, baubles and streamers.

'Wherever did you get those lovely decorations?' Olga asked.

'I was given them when the English church in Rome had to close down,' Betty explained.

From the same source there were candles which, lit and put in nooks and crannies all over the house, made it look like an enchanted castle, in which the smallest child cast a huge shadow on the wall. In this flickering, twinkling candlelight the children romped and sang all the carols they could remember.

They even had a turkey, given to them by the de Marchis. This Betty insisted on cooking herself, much to Serafina's indignation.

'If I leave it to her,' she confided to Olga Sabatini, 'she'll cut it into tiny pieces and frizzle them up so that no one gets a decent piece of meat.'

'It will be interesting to see the English way of cooking it,' Olga replied diplomatically. Having persuaded Serafina to accept her as a legitimate sharer of the precious kitchen, she was not going to risk taking sides on such an important matter as cooking the Christmas dinner.

There were many hilarious afternoons at the de Marchis' house or their own at which huge parties of grown-ups and children played the old nursery games, sardines, up-Jenkins, harkee, seekers on the stairs, hide and seek, musical chairs, and of course bingo, which is the traditional Italian pastime at Christmas.

So, despite war, anxiety and privation, they managed to enjoy themselves.

On New Year's Day 1944 Umbria was still snow-bound. The burning question was, of course, how soon they would be liberated. They realised that they could not expect an Allied offensive during the present freeze-up, but most people were sure the 'big push' would come in the spring.

Betty also had to face the ever present problem of how to make ends meet. The Sabatini's rent paid only for the bare necessities of life and she had already made every economy she could think of. Reluctantly, she decided that she would have to give Serafina notice.

'But, Signora, you know you need not pay me any wages,' the maid protested.

'Oh, nonsense, I can't let you work for me for nothing.'

'All I want is my food, if you can afford it, and my room – and that's not nothing, Signora.'

Betty tried another argument. 'You might be safer if you weren't living in an Englishwoman's house. You know what the Germans and fascists are like. Guilt by association is part of their creed.'

'All the same, I feel safest with you. Whatever happens, I want to stay.'

In the end, touched by Serafina's loyalty and affection, Betty had to agree, hoping she would be able to make it up to her after the war.

After much thought, Betty decided to start giving English lessons again. There proved to be no difficulty in finding pupils. Although the schools were still closed, parents were keen that their children should carry on with their studies, and English was a popular subject, especially if it could be taught clandestinely.

Later a strange assortment of adults also applied for lessons. The first applicant was Rocco, the grocer's assistant. Betty soon found out he could barely read or write Italian, let alone English.

'Why do you want to learn?' she asked him.

'I thought it would be easier to get a job with the Allies when they come, Signora.' A heartening sentiment.

Alfio, the electrician, came ostensibly for the same reason, but partly also, Betty suspected, to resume his on-and-off courtship of Serafina who, however, treated him cavalierly. In her constant search for eligible and susceptible males, Serafina too was eagerly awaiting the arrival of the English soldiers and, even more, their rich American comrades-in-arms.

The next to apply were two of the hairdresser's girls, though possibly they did not envisage getting jobs in the hairdressing line.

One evening Mario, the Captain of Carabinieri, arrived in civilian clothes. His grandmother had been English so he knew the language fairly well.

'I have to keep in with the Germans because my job depends on that,' he explained, 'but I long for the Allies to arrive.'

Three times a week he made his way up to the house by devious routes as he did not want anyone to know where he was going.

One day he arrived in great good humour, bearing a bottle of sparkling wine, which he presented to Betty.

'What are we celebrating Mario?, Your birthday?'

'No, Signora. I have brought off a small victory against the enemy.'

'That's clever of you,' Betty said as they clinked glasses. 'How?'

'Well, we got an order from the Germans to lead them up into the mountains near Norcia to arrest some partisans and escaped prisoners.'

'How did they know where to look?'

'An informer had given away their hiding place. I know who it was and he'll be dealt with when the Allies come.'

'So what did you do?'

'I had to send off a squad of Carabinieri to lead the Germans, of course. But at the same time I sent two of my men, disguised in peasant clothes, by the direct route across the mountains to warn the partisans. By the time the Germans arrived they had all dispersed.'

'You must have great faith in your men, Mario,' Betty said. 'If the Germans had found out they would have shot you, wouldn't they?'

'We all hate the Germans. None of us is a fascist.'

One Saturday morning early in March Betty was preparing a simple English lesson for Rocco, the grocer's boy, when Serafina came in to tell her that a Signora Pellicioli was at the front door and would like to see her. Betty knew no one of that name, but told the maid to show her in.

Her visitor was an extremely pretty young woman, smartly dressed in a bright red suit, with beautifully coiffeured chestnut coloured hair, a shapely figure and long legs encased in black silk stockings. She advanced confidently into the room and greeted Betty with a friendly smile.

'I see you are busy, Contessa. I'm exceedingly sorry to disturb you.'

Betty waved her to a chair. 'What can I do for you, Signora?'

'My name is Anna Pellicioli. I am the wife of Dr Cesare Pellicioli. He works at the hospital and we have a flat nearby.' She paused, then said dramatically: 'I have come to see you because I am a coward.'

Betty was mystified, as she supposed her visitor intended her to be. She decided not to make the obvious reply. Instead, she said with a faint smile: 'You don't look like the popular conception of a coward.'

Signora Pellicioli was in no way abashed.

'Oh, but I am, I assure you, Contessa. I'm terrified of these dreadful air raids. Not only that, but I can't sleep for fear of the bombs. I'm becoming a physical and mental wreck.'

Betty thought she did not look at all like that either, but did not say so.

'So you see I've got to get out of the town before I crack up altogether. A patient of Cesare's told him that you might have accommodation to let. Now you see why I'm here disturbing you at your work.'

Comparing the extroverted Anna Pellicioli with the quiet, reserved Olga Sabatini, Betty was struck by the thought that the raids had had the same effect on two such opposite types. She would soon find herself keeping a hostel for the bomb-shy. However, she did need all the extra money she could get.

'My balcony room is empty, Signora. It's been too cold to use, but now, I hope, the worst of the winter is over. You can have that if you like.'

Anna leapt to her feet, arms outstretched, as if she were about to embrace her benefactress.

'Oh how wonderful! I shall be grateful to you for as long as I live.'

'Don't you want to see it?'

'I'm sure it will be perfect. Cesare is off duty at lunchtime. Could we move in this afternoon, do you think, Signora?'

Betty was disarmed by her joy. 'I suppose you could, but it probably needs cleaning. I'll try to get Serafina to do it straight away.'

'Oh no, don't do that. I'll clean it myself. I shall be a model tenant, I promise you.'

Thanking Betty again profusely, Anna rushed off to tell her husband the glad news.

Cesare proved to be a tall sombre man, pleasant but with no small talk. The gay and glamorous Anna, however, soon became friends with everyone, even Serafina, who was impressed by her sincere efforts not to give the maid any extra work. She played happily with the children and listened, apparently enthralled, to the Maresciallo's long and boring stories. Despite her fear of the bombs, she seemed to take life as a huge joke.

Cesare worked all day at the hospital and if there were no signs of aircraft overhead Anna often went with him, so they had their meals out, thus relieving pressure in the kitchen. On his return Cesare usually looked tired and depressed, but one evening when Betty opened the front door to let him in he appeared utterly exhausted.

He plumped his black bag on the floor and sighed.

'It's becoming impossible, Contessa. We're short of everything – drugs, medicines, dressings – everything. We have hardly any anaesthetics and many of our patients we have to send home. The urgent ones we sometimes have to operate on without anaesthetics. It's a nightmare.'

At the end of April the Allied air raids were intensified and planes passed overhead almost every day. They could hear the bombing of Terni, where the hydro-electric works, the steel works and the arms factory were all hit.

The boys would dash out, yelling and waving to the American bombers as they passed comparatively low over Colle Attivoli, but Betty had to try to suppress their shouts of joy, thinking that such sentiments would not endear them to the Germans or to any Italians with friends or relatives living near the Allied targets.

Early one morning the planes came over, dropped a few bombs and then flew off in the direction of Terni. About an hour later, just as they were beginning breakfast, there was a tremendous explosion. The house rocked and several windows at the back were shattered.

Alec, carrying his precious boiled egg from the saucepan to the kitchen table, was flung across the room, smashing his egg on the opposite wall, and the other children were thrown off their seats. When they had all recovered from the shock, Betty remembered Olga Sabatini and ran up to her room.

Olga was lying face down on the bed, a blanket pulled up to her neck and her hands pressed over her ears. She was trembling and did not hear Betty enter until she spoke gently.

'It's all right, Olga. It wasn't very near, I don't think, even though it made such an awful blast. The planes have gone now.'

Olga turned over slowly and sat up.

'God, oh God! What about Sabatino? He's at the barracks. He may be dead.'

It was no good to let her lie there, imagining the worst, Betty decided. She took Olga by the hand and helped her to her feet.

'We'll take a look from the other side.'

When they got down all the peasants and the children were gathered in front of the house, gazing down on Spoleto where a huge column of smoke and flames was rising into the still air. It seemed to come from beyond the lower end of the town.

'It's nowhere near the barracks anyway,' Betty pointed out to Olga, glad that she had made her come down.

That evening Mario, the Captain of Carabinieri, came for his English lesson and was able to tell them what had happened.

'It was the station. There was a munitions train standing in a siding – that's what they were after, of course. The bombs hit some of the rolling stock, which caught fire. They tried to put it out before it reached the munitions train, but they failed.' Mario sounded rather gleeful.

Betty asked if there had been much loss of life.

'Remarkably little. The station was flattened, of course, but as you know it's quite a way from the town.'

When later that evening Cesare returned safely from the hospital he confirmed that the casualties had been surprisingly light.

'Five killed, including three Germans, I'm told. And I had to tend only about half a dozen slightly injured people. We were expecting much worse.'

'How about poor Anna?' Betty asked. 'She must have been terrified.'

Cesare smiled. 'By some miracle she had been offered a lift to Assisi in one of our ambulances. She has an aunt there and she had arranged to stay the night.'

This was the only serious raid on Spoleto.

Betty had had no news of Valentino for over a year and she could not bear to think of the danger he must be in if, as she believed, he had joined the partisans in the north. She knew too that the greatest danger was still to come, when the partisans would launch their fiercest onslaught against the retreating Germans after the Allies had got them on the run.

The few notes that had come from her mother through the Red Cross via Switzerland had ceased and she felt very much alone. The future seemed menacing in the extreme and there was little one could do to prepare for the unknown.

She took Enrico and Alec aside and told them they must all be ready for any crisis.

'You realise that if anything happens to me you will have to take over and make sure Billy and Teresa are safe.'

Enrico looked worried. 'If they arrested you, Mum, they'll probably pull me in with you, and possibly Alec as well. What then?'

Betty had been thinking, not so much of arrest, as of becoming a casualty of the battle when it passed over them, but she did not say so. In any case the problem was the same.

She had had one idea which she now proceeded to put into effect. She made the children learn by heart the names, addresses and telephone numbers of her mother, brother and aunts in England.

They would recite one after another:

Mrs Keatinge Johnson
9 Clarendon Road
Tunbridge Wells
Telephone number: Tunbridge Wells 5786

Miss Olive Brodribb
3 Southwell Gardens
Knightsbridge
London
Telephone number: Sloane 2391

At least if something happened to her or if they were separated, they would know how to contact the family.

On 6 June 1944 the Allies took Rome and the Germans started withdrawing north. Betty felt sure the crucial moment was coming and knew they might be overwhelmed by a retreating army using 'scorched earth' tactics. In case they had to make a sudden dash into the nearby woods, she prepared knapsacks, one for each of them, containing essential clothing, waterproofs, rations and a few tools.

On the night of 16 June they went to bed as usual, but at midnight came the sound that Betty had long been dreading – the pounding of a rifle butt on the front door. Her bedroom window looked directly on to the courtyard. She leapt out of bed and flung open the shutters. In the moonlight she could see half a dozen Germans with an enormous lorry outside the gate.

The soldier who had been banging heard the window, looked up and shouted in Italian: 'Open up at once. Who is the owner of this house?'

Trying to stop her voice trembling, Betty answered: 'I am.'

'Then come down and open immediately.'

She threw some clothes on, ran downstairs and unbolted the door.

Without preamble the soldier said: 'We need this house. So all get out.'

Determined not to show how terrified she was, Betty summoned up her reserves of courage.

'You can't have my house. It's already full. I've got three families and several children, including the family of a maresciallo in the Italian Army. We can't have military here as well.'

The German looked non-plussed. He had probably never been addressed like this by an Italian householder, let alone a woman. Before he could think what to say, Betty told him, untruly as it happened, that when she agreed to house the Maresciallo's family she had been assured that no one else would be billeted on her.

'Go further up the hill and you'll probably find some empty villa more suitable for you.'

He thought for a moment.

'Very well, we'll go and look, but we'll probably be back. You will prepare accommodation for us.'

Perhaps aware that he had not come too well out of this exchange, he added loudly with a glance over his shoulder at his comrades standing round the lorry: 'And that's an order.'

Then they all piled into the lorry, which trundled off up the hill.

By this time, of course, the whole household was awake. Serafina was tearing her hair. 'They won't find anything up the hill, Signora. They're bound to come back. *Che disastro*!'

'Anyway, we've got a breathing space,' Betty said. 'The first thing we must do is get rid of anything that looks English.'

In five minutes the house was in chaos as they all set to work, feverishly piling English books and papers into boxes and cases, flinging them on top of wardrobes, under beds, outside the back door, and even down the well. From this last hiding place the books were never, alas, recovered.

They had hardly finished when back came the Germans. They crowded into the hall, headed by an N.C.O. who was evidently in charge of them. He looked surly but spoke excellent Italian.

'We have found nowhere as suitable as your house. We are moving in straight away.'

This time, Betty saw, there was no hope of keeping them out. She could only try to compromise.

'As I told one of your men, the house is full. However, you can have the ground floor and we'll live upstairs.'

To her surprise he agreed with a curt nod. 'Any men in your household will help to unload the lorry.'

So Sabatino and Enrico went with the soldiers and carried arms, cases of ammunition and all sorts of equipment into the dining room.

Informed of the German order by a breathless Serafina, Doctor Pellicioli refused to help. In fact he did not appear at all, but Anna was in her element, revelling in all the excitement and attracting admiring glances from the German soldiers. She cracked jokes with the children until their tense expressions gradually relaxed and they began to smile.

The German N.C.O., whom one of his men addressed as Emmanuel, stood just inside the front door supervising the unloading. Large and red-faced, with an overbearing manner, he was nevertheless obviously well educated, and as she looked at him standing there Betty seemed to discern behind his arrogant façade a disillusioned and very exhausted young man.

On an impulse she went up to him and said: 'You look so tired. Would you like a cup of coffee?'

In an instant his whole attitude changed. As he looked at her he smiled for the first time. 'That is kind of you, but I will wait until my men have finished their job and then we will brew our own coffee. We mustn't use yours.'

Betty had no reason to regret her impulsive action, because during their stay in the house the Germans behaved most correctly and treated everyone with courtesy. They had their own camp beds which they arranged in the sitting room and dining room, amongst all their equipment, and in the hall. After they had settled in and eaten their meal, cooked in the kitchen with Serafina looking on disapprovingly but too scared to protest, most of them went off to explore the town while Betty and her children finished clearing out the English books and hiding them more efficiently.

Next morning the family handyman Gino arrived. They had been walling off part of the cellar in which to hide some of their belongings – bicycles, cameras, sewing machines, a typewriter and anything else that they thought of value. The wall was only half erected and Gino was preparing the mortar to finish the job when Betty heard Emmanuel calling for her. She ran quickly up the cellar stairs, closing the door at the top.

With a day and night's rest, some of the burly N.C.O.'s arrogance seemed to have returned. 'I want to see over the house. You will accompany me.'

Anna appeared at Betty's side. She raised a pair of black-pencilled eyebrows at Emmanuel. 'Do we look like partisans?'

The German pretended not to have heard her. Betty led him to the top of the house and showed him the ladder to the attic which he proceeded to climb.

'He's going to stick his nose into everything,' she whispered to Anna.

She took as long as possible showing him the bedrooms, hoping that by the time he returned to the ground floor he would have had enough. But when he got to the cellar door he asked where it led to.

'Only the cellar.'

'I will inspect it.'

At the bottom of the stairs he discovered Gino, cowering by the half-completed wall, clutching his mortar trowel and looking petrified. Emmanuel peered into the hole. 'Here, what's this?'

With great presence of mind Anna answered: 'Oh, we are just going to hide a few things here in case the Americans arrive. We hear they help themselves to anything they fancy.'

Emmanuel roared with laughter. 'If the Americans ever come – which I doubt – they will find that our S.S. troops have already made a clean sweep. However, go on walling it up and I'll come and look at it when it's finished.'

So Gino, who by this time had decided that the Germans must be as mad as the English, went on with his work, shaking his head in bewilderment.

When he had closed up the hole, Emmanuel returned and examined it critically. 'That fresh paint is very obvious. It must be properly hidden.'

Calling two of his soldiers, he told them to camouflage the wall. So Gino and the Germans set to with a will, throwing mud at the wall and piling brushwood against it until no one could tell there was a little room behind.

In fact it was found neither by S.S. troops nor by Americans, and later they retrieved everything intact.

Gradually they adapted themselves to military occupation and to living crowded on top of each other on the first floor.

The Germans had 'won' a sheep from somewhere. They slaughtered the poor creature in the courtyard and hung it in the doorway to drip. Betty kept the children out of the way during these gory proceedings, but later they were glad to accept a joint of mutton to help eke out their meagre rations.

Having apparently lost touch with their rear echelon, the Germans too were very short of food. Betty would find them in the kitchen boiling up a few potatoes and cabbage leaves to make soup, and this seemed to be all they had. They gave very little trouble. They were out all day, leaving a couple of sentries on the house, and in the evenings they listened to their own battery wireless by the light of an acetylene lamp. The power station at Terni had been blown up and, having very few candles, the families on the first floor just went to bed when it got dark.

One morning Emmanuel stopped Betty as she was coming downstairs on her way to the garden. Speaking in his precise and grammatical Italian, he told her that his soldiers wanted to take a bath that afternoon.

'They have gathered enough firewood to heat water on the stove.'

'All right,' Betty said, 'I'll tell everyone to keep clear of the bathroom after lunch.'

She started to descend the last two stairs but Emmanuel did not step aside to let her pass. Instead he said in excellent English: 'I've been meaning to ask you: where is your husband?'

Betty had the presence of mind to look at him blankly and reply in Italian: '*Scusi, cosa diceva?*'

Emmanuel smiled ruefully and did not press her. She knew he suspected her of being English, and every now and then he would repeat his trick of suddenly shooting a question at her in her native tongue. She had to be careful not to reply.

School had started again when the weather got warmer, but now the children were already on holiday – the long summer holidays of over three months which parents found so exhausting. Betty started a timetable of lessons to keep them out of mischief. Teresa spent most of her time playing with the peasant children, in particular her great friend Clelia, who was of the same age and a sweet, gentle little girl.

Some of the boys' friends still came up to the house. They continued to build their fortifications in the garden, a strong palisade with a deep trench in front of it. This trench was found useful by the Germans. When the planes came over, two or three of them had room to cower there under cover, much to the boys' amusement.

On 25 June Betty was woken by a great deal of bustle and shouting from downstairs. Looking out of her window, she saw that the Germans' lorry had been backed through the front gate and into the courtyard. Soldiers were loading arms, crates of ammunition and equipment. They seemed to be in a great hurry. From what she had heard of the news Betty guessed that they had been told to withdraw quickly so as not to be caught in a pincer movement by the Allies.

She dressed and went downstairs. Emmanuel beckoned to her. 'We are going immediately. You have treated us with kindness which I shall not forget.' He was fumbling in his pocket. 'Here is some money which you may need. Go and change it at the Kommandatur. Then go into hiding in the hills. It is better for you not to be here when the S.S. troops come, after us.'

He was pressing some notes into her hand.

'I can't let you give me money,' she said. 'Will you take some pictures in return?'

He looked delighted and chose some large watercolours. After he had said goodbye to the boys he bent down to Teresa and whispered: 'How English everything smells in this house! Why, even the little one is painting in an English drawing book!'

He put his hands on Betty's shoulders and said: 'You have been good to us. I shall come and see you after the war.'

Then he added, in English, 'Goodbye' – and laughed.

With the departure of the Germans Betty found herself overcome by inertia, by a reluctance to start getting to grips immediately with the dilemma that now faced them.

After occupying Rome on 6 June the Allies had evidently paused to consolidate, but she knew it would not be long before they resumed their advance. She imagined the Army marching along the Via Flaminia, the Roman road from Rome, to liberate Spoleto – flags flying, drums beating – and she wanted so much to be at home with her children to witness this momentous occasion. Meanwhile, however, they were threatened by the retreating Germans, and Spoleto was on one of the direct routes north.

Gradually, as it dawned on them that the house was their own again, that they need not think twice before every word they uttered, the normal noisy routine of life at Casa San Marzano returned, with the boys shouting and rushing around the house and garden. But as soon as this natural reaction to the strained atmosphere of the last few weeks simmered down, Betty knew that she must face up to the urgent problem of what to do next.

In the evenings, when the children were in bed, the adults congregated in the kitchen where they would conduct an unending and inconclusive debate, Sabatino looking glum with little Fiorella asleep in his arms, Cesare standing aloof in a corner, and Anna ready to argue about anything at the top of her voice. Olga, whose nerves had been badly shaken by the air raids and the Germans, was also vociferous and put forward all sorts of impossible suggestions which were immediately slapped down by Anna. Sometimes the high-pitched altercations were so noisy that Enrico and Alec would wake, come down and join in until their mother packed them off to bed again and told the adults it was time they all got some sleep.

Eventually each family solved the problem in a different way.

Cesare and Anna Pellicioli decided to return to Spoleto. The Doctor was still extremely busy at the hospital, and living on the premises would at least save him the journey to and from Colle Attivoli every day. Now that the Germans had withdrawn from the town the danger of Allied air raids had receded, at least until the retreating forces began to pass through the area.

Anna's terror of the bombing had, however, been replaced by another obsession, the fear of starving, as Betty found out when she went to see her in her room prior to their departure. Against the far wall of the bedroom stood row upon row of tins containing foods of every description. Betty's eyes opened wide.

'Good heavens, Anna! Where on earth did you get all those?'

Anna looked slightly guilty, but defiant. 'Everything's disappearing, Betty. I believe before it's over we shan't be able to buy as much as a crust of bread.'

'But if we all hoarded like that there wouldn't be anything in the shops now.'

'I dare say it's selfish and wrong, but I have to think of Cesare, don't I? What would his patients do if he collapsed from lack of food?'

Despite her obsessive fears, however, Betty knew from the way in which she had faced up to their various crises, including the alarming occasion when the Germans had arrived to take over the house, that Anna was by no means lacking in courage. Her exuberance and irrepressible high spirits had so often helped them through their moments of depression. The children adored her and even Serafina tried to persuade her to stay. Cesare, with his kindly gentleness, was just as well liked, and Betty was sorry to see them go.

The day after their departure Billy came out with a rash on his legs and Betty went down to the hospital to see if Dr Pellicioli could provide some healing ointment.

'Where's Anna?' she asked him as he spooned some white cream out of a big jar into a carton.

'We managed to find a room for her here.'

'Could I say hullo to her before I leave?'

'Of course, Betty.'

He shepherded her out of his surgery and led her towards the other end of the hospital, stopping as he turned into a long, straight corridor. 'You'll find her in the last room but one on the left.'

Betty's first knock yielded no reply. She knocked again. An anxious voice from inside asked who was there.

'Only me. Betty.'

'Oh, come in. What a pleasant surprise.'

Anna was sitting up in bed, wearing a pink silk nightie with a deeply plunging neckline.

'Oh dear,' Betty said, 'Cesare didn't tell me you were ill.'

'I'm not.'

Seeing Betty looking non-plussed, she went on: 'You remember the first time I met you I told you I was a coward?' Betty nodded. 'Well, I've decided to stay here in bed until those beastly Germans pass through and the Allies arrive.'

The Allies had an unexpected delight in store for them when they took over the hospital, Betty thought, eyeing Anna's splendid curves jutting over the top of the bedclothes. Then she noticed some odd shapes sticking up at the other end of the bed.

'What ever have you got down there, Anna?'

Anna laughed and pulled down the bedclothes. Arrayed around and between her legs were her precious tins of food.

Next day the Maresciallo sought out Betty and told her he had decided to follow Dr Pellicioli's example and move back to Spoleto.

'I'm on duty every day at the barracks,' he explained, 'and there are permanent quarters for me there. It seems a waste of time to trek back and forth here now that the Germans have pulled out and the bombing's stopped.'

'What about your family?' Betty asked.

'The women will have to make up their own minds.'

This they had great difficulty in doing. Aunt Eugenia was in favour of returning to Spoleto, but Olga was still fearful of the bombing. In the end she persuaded Eugenia to stay at Colle Attivoli.

One morning after breakfast Teresa came running to her mother, a worried expression on her face. 'Mummy, I think there's something the matter with Caterina. She looks awful.'

Betty followed her to the stable. The little donkey stood with her head drooping, her eyes half closed and one of them oozing.

Teresa pointed to one full haybag hanging above the manger. 'She hasn't even eaten her supper.'

'You're right. She doesn't look very well,' Betty said. 'I'd better fetch Tonino.'

'I'll come with you, Mummy.'

Tonino, the vet, lived on the far side of Spoleto. It was a long walk for a five-year-old, but Betty knew that if Teresa was left behind she would only stay with her beloved donkey, brooding and worrying.

'Come on then. We'll go straight away. I'll ask Serafina to see to the lunch.'

They reached the vet's house about midday, only to find he was out. His cheerful wife insisted on their waiting and ushered them into the *salotto*, the room which in nearly all Italian working-class houses is smartly furnished and hardly ever used. This one contained a wide variety of stuffed animals under glass cases. Teresa looked at them with a mixture of curiosity and horror. 'Where did he get them all, Mummy? Did he kill them?'

'I've no idea, darling,' said Betty untruthfully.

Fortunately at that moment Tonino walked in. He had a van for which he had managed to get some black market petrol, and much to Betty's relief he drove them back to Casa San Marzano.

He examined Caterina carefully without saying anything, then asked Teresa to get him some hot water from the kitchen. When she had gone he turned to Betty with a rueful smile. 'I'm afraid she's a gonner. When a donkey falls ill like this one, it seems to give up the ghost. No matter what you do, she just won't try to get better. They're proper fatalists, donkeys are.'

'Oh dear, Teresa will be heartbroken.'

'For the little girl's sake, I'll give her some medicine, but it won't do any good. She'll be gone by the morning, you can take it from me.'

He bathed the donkey's eyes with the warm water Teresa had brought, poured some red fluid from a bottle down her throat and then departed.

Next morning Betty woke early, dressed quickly and went down to the stable. Alas, Tonino had been right. Caterina was stretched out on the straw, dead.

Betty roused the boys and they dragged the carcase down to the orchard where they dug a grave for her under an apple tree.

Then Betty turned back to the house, nerving herself to break the sad news to Teresa.

That evening Betty and the boys listened to the B.B.C. news as usual. The Allies had resumed their offensive and were pushing north.

The decision whether to stay put or go into hiding could be postponed no longer. With the Sabatini family, Olga, Eugenia and the two small girls, they would be a party of nine this time, making it more difficult to find a refuge. Partly for this reason Olga was in favour of sitting it out, but Betty thought they would be safer in the countryside. The question was: where?

Since their return from Roselli, Enrico, Alec and their friends had made several trips into the surrounding hills and forests in the hope of meeting up with more escaped British prisoners-of-war or Italian partisans. In this they had not succeeded, but they now knew the terrain very well.

'Mummy,' Alec said suddenly, 'do you remember that evening last week when we were late for supper?'

Betty nodded.

'Well, we had gone further than we meant to, of course, but we came on a tiny village called Monte le Rossi. We were with Marcello and Virgilio, but none of us knew it even existed, did we, Enrico?'

'It's only a hamlet really,' Enrico said, 'but it's a long way from the town and there's no road to it.'

Betty thought it sounded promising. 'First thing tomorrow morning you had better go and reconnoitre it and see if there's anywhere we could lie up for a few days.'

Enrico and Alec were off before dawn and returned in time for a late lunch. They had found an empty barn.

'Better still,' Enrico said, 'there's no sign of Jerry anywhere.'

They agreed to set off for Monte le Rossi next morning and Olga decided to join them with her children, but at the last minute Eugenia opted out. 'I don't want to be alone when the Germans pass through,' she said, 'but I've got friends in Spoleto who have offered to put me up and I think I'll go there.'

Eugenia had been good at amusing the smaller children, who would miss her.

After much asking around, they managed to borrow a handcart on to which they loaded as much as they could – sleeping bags, tools, utensils and food. Fortunately, as it was summer, they did not need to take blankets or much in the way of clothes.

They knew that the path up to the village was steep and stony and that, without a donkey, they would all have to do their share of pushing and pulling. Amid considerable confusion, excitement and laughter they eventually got going.

Their mood was very different to that of their previous flight. They were filled with optimism, knowing that deliverance was at hand and they only had to survive for the next few days.

They soon found, however, that they needed all their energy and endurance to haul the cart up that very precipitous path. The journey could only have been about four miles, but the cart seemed to get heavier and heavier and the path steeper and steeper, and it felt more like forty miles. They had only one brief respite when they were asked in for refreshment at a farmhouse whose owner the boys knew.

The journey took the whole day and when at last Monte le Rossi hove in sight, nestling among the woods in a fold in the hills, they all cheered and drank their last drop of wine. Another hour's hard labour was needed before they finally staggered into the hamlet to a kind reception from the villagers. Quite a deputation, mainly of grubby children, conducted them to the empty, broken-down barn at the edge of the hamlet.

There were not more than a dozen houses and a tiny chapel. The whole place had an air of dire poverty. Apart from the children only elderly women were to be seen with a look of despair on their faces.

The newcomers and their strange baggage train provided a most welcome distraction for the children, who stood around entranced while they unloaded and tried to arrange their few possessions in their new home. There was plenty of rather dirty straw, which would do well for a communal bed. For their evening meal the villagers brought them some bread and fruit. Then they threw themselves down on the straw, utterly exhausted.

Next day they explored the village and made friends with the inhabitants. One family was especially friendly. Emilia, the old grandmother, who seemed to be paralysed, sat immovable all day on a chair at the top of the steps leading to her kitchen. She had a lovely mischievous, toothless grin and Betty felt very drawn towards her. Every evening her son Raffo came home from Spoleto, where he worked, and he and his wife seemed disposed to help them in every way, even letting them cook their own soup over the wood fire.

They found that the younger women drove the cattle up into the woods every morning, because both the Germans and the fascists were apt to make lightning raids on the village, taking anything they could, including livestock.

On the second morning Betty said: 'Come on, I think we'd better follow the cows into hiding. We don't want to have to explain what we are doing here to Jerries or fascists.'

They camouflaged their belongings in the barn and made their way up the hillside to the edge of the woods, from which they could keep an eye on any happenings in the hamlet below.

For the Italian peasants, caught up in a war that was none of their making, tranquillity could turn to outrage in a matter of minutes.

June is one of the most beautiful months of the year in Umbria, and Betty and her children had spent a warm and cloudless day exploring the woods surrounding their new home. About midday they had come upon a clearing where they could lie on their backs and bask in the sun, gazing up at the blue sky above.

After a few minutes rest Teresa got to her feet and wandered off, and the others were still soaking up the sunshine when they heard her call: 'I say, look what I've found!'

She ran back to her mother and opened her right hand to reveal two or three beautifully ripe though slightly squashed wild strawberries.

'You clever darling,' Betty said as the strawberries disappeared rapidly into Teresa's mouth.

The boys leapt to their feet and rushed over to where Teresa had called from.

Alec whooped with joy. 'There are hundreds of them.'

The plants, growing prolifically between the stumps of the felled trees, were loaded with fruit. After they had gorged themselves for a few minutes, Betty suggested that they should pick what remained into a carton so that they would have a luxury dessert to follow their frugal lunch of cold pasta and bread.

In the evening, pleased with life and themselves after an idyllic day, they paused as usual just inside the wood before going down to the barn for the night.

Betty and Valentino on their wedding day, 28 October 1927.

Enrico, Alec, Billy and Teresa at the Casa San Marzano.

Betty.

Valentino in uniform.

Marshal Badoglio announcing the Armistice with the Allies in September 1943. With him is Brigadier General Maxwell Taylor of the U.S. Army.

The Casa San Marzano, with Spoleto in the background.

Allied troops advancing through an Italian village.

An Allied soldier chatting to Italian children during the advance through Italy.

A motley band of partisans fighting on the side of the Allies.

Betty, after the War.

Enrico pointed to the doors of two stalls which were still standing open. 'The girls don't seem to have brought the cattle back yet. I wonder why.'

A moment later several of the elderly women appeared in the little village square, talking excitedly and gesticulating. The children clung close to them, clutching at their hands. Then they all turned and fell silent as half a dozen black-shirted fascists, sub-machine-guns at the ready, emerged from one of the narrow streets, driving before them a bowed figure in a grey suit.

When they got to the centre of the square the man turned and faced the fascists, apparently protesting or entreating. The blackshirts took no notice but continued to threaten their captive with their guns. The man made frantic gestures apparently indicating innocence or helplessness.

Then two of the fascists left the others, crossed the square again and entered a house in the street from which they had first appeared. A moment later a woman and three children staggered out with the fascists urging them forward towards the group on the square. When she reached them the woman flung her arms round the man's neck, her shoulders heaving as she sobbed. The children took shelter behind her skirts.

The fascists pulled them roughly apart and proceeded to line the whole family up against the far wall of the square. Three of them then cocked their guns and pointed them at the five cowering figures.

'My God, Mummy, they're going to shoot them,' Enrico whispered.

The man fell to his knees and started to gabble, making frantic gestures at the men pointing the guns. Amid a terrible scene of screaming and panic the fascists yanked the man to his feet and frogmarched him across the square towards the chapel. In abject terror his wife and children collapsed against the wall, their heads buried beneath their arms.

Outside the chapel the fascists halted and again rammed the muzzles of their guns into the man's back. He lurched forward, then gave a feeble wave towards the roof.

Two of the fascists disappeared, returning a few minutes later carrying a ladder which they leant against the wall of the chapel. Soon they had climbed on to the roof and started hurling down tiles, regardless of the women still standing below who beat a hasty retreat. Apparently not finding what they were looking for, they shouted angrily to their comrades, one of whom stuck his gun against the back of their captive's neck. The terrified man must have given further directions, for the two on the roof moved further up and hurled more tiles to the ground. At last one of them gave a triumphant cry and hauled out three packages which he held aloft, to cheers from the fascists below. The searchers climbed quickly down and the captive was released with a kick to speed him on his way. The fascists then shouldered their arms and made off, obviously anxious to get well clear of the village before darkness fell.

To make quite sure it was safe to return, Betty and the children waited until they saw the young women leading the cattle down the hillside from the woods, but even when they reached the derelict barn it no longer seemed the safe refuge that it had been that morning.

Betty realised that she could not expect to be given a coherent account of what had happened until the inhabitants of Monte le Rossi had had time to recover from the shock of the fascists' villainy. Trying to remain calm herself, she gave the children their supper and put the two younger ones to bed. She waited until they were asleep before setting off with Enrico and Alec to find Raffo at Emilia's house. Still shaken by the events of the afternoon, the old woman murmured over and over again: '*Che disastro*!'

Betty put a sympathetic hand on Emilia's shoulder, then turned to Raffo: 'Who was that poor man they were threatening?'

'His name is Mellini. He's a tailor in Spoleto.'

'Oh, I remember his shop now. He's rather well-to-do, isn't he?'

Raffo smiled ruefully. 'Let's say he was, poor wretch. He's not worth ten lire now.'

Betty waited for him to explain and he went on: 'Mellini was the smartest tailor in Spoleto and he made a good living, but he always maintained that the lira would be worth nothing after the war. He used to say this to everyone, and his views probably didn't endear him to the fascists.'

'So what did he do, then?'

'Apart from what he kept to live on, he converted all his profits into gold and silver ornaments and jewellery. The trouble was that too many people knew what he was doing.'

'But how did the fascists know that he had fled to Monte le Rossi?'

'They must have had a tip-off. They didn't know where he had hidden his valuables, of course. Hence the pretty scene you witnessed on the square.'

'Poor Mellini.'

'Yes, to quote Pagliacci: "*La comedia è finita*,"' said Raffo, who was an ardent opera fan.

The very next morning, after an agitated and restless night, they were woken at dawn by guttural shouts of '*Raus*! *Raus*!'

They stumbled to their feet, brushing off whisps of straw. They had no nightwear with them so had no need to dress, but hastily pulled on their clogs or shoes.

Betty thought to herself: 'It's unbelievable. This tiny hamlet in the back of beyond, yet we suffer the fascists yesterday and the Germans today. We should have stayed at home. It couldn't have been worse than this.'

She peered out of the barn door, hoping they could slip up the field and into the woods, but discerned a steel-helmeted figure with fixed bayonet barring the way to their sanctuary. From the sound of their voices Betty realised that the Germans had started their search at the top of the village, but had posted a sentry at the other end to cut off any retreat.

She quickly gathered up her documents, then turned to her eldest son: 'I'm going to find Emilia and get her to hide these for me.'

She reached Emilia's house without being spotted. The old woman was over eighty, but she was extremely quick on the uptake. She gave Betty her toothy grin, took the papers and stuffed them away under her voluminous skirts. Betty ran back as fast as she could and was still panting when three or four Jerries pushed their way into the barn.

They looked exhausted, ill-tempered and unkempt. Without a word they proceeded to pull apart the bedding and empty knapsacks upside down, scattering devastation everywhere. Both families' precious store of food, including their carefully hoarded chocolate, was seized, but while they were busy looting the food, Alec managed to extract the bayonet that he had in his baggage and push it through a crack in the wall.

Out of the corner of her eye Betty was watching this hazardous operation, but when she turned back to the Germans she saw that the most aggressive and least prepossessing member of the group was looking closely at one of the sheets of paper in which their stores were wrapped.

He beckoned her over. 'What is this?'

When Valentino was at Staff College he had written a series of theses on the Napoleonic Wars. In the loft at Casa San Marzano there was a huge boxful of these typewritten works. Betty was not sure, however, whether it was politic to disclose that her husband was an Italian Army officer, and a regular one at that. Relations between the former allies were now about as bad as they could be, and the Germans tended to regard all Italians, and particularly the armed forces, as traitors. She therefore hesitated before replying.

'Well, what is it?' the German persisted.

'My grandfather was a military historian,' she told him. 'He wrote a book on the Napoleonic Wars. These sheets are part of the original manuscript.'

'But why have you got them here with you?'

'Because paper is extremely scarce. We use that stuff for everything. Even toilet paper,' she added, smiling hopefully at him, but all he did was frown at this disclosure of one of their domestic improvisations.

'You will have to come down to our headquarters with us and explain – if you can.'

'That's absurd. It's completely harmless. Can't you understand, it's all about things that happened over a hundred years ago.'

The German went on peering at the sheet of paper in his hand. Evidently he had some knowledge of the Italian language, for he called the two Jerries standing nearest to him to his side. 'You see this. It says something about withdrawal.'

The other two Germans gazed down at the typescript, trying to look perceptive, but as far as they were concerned it might as well have been written in Chinese.

'It's probably a passage about Napoleon's retreat from Moscow,' Betty murmured. 'Well, I suppose you might glean something useful from that.'

The suspicious German picked up another typewritten sheet and began trying to read it. Suddenly, he fixed her with an angry glare. 'How are we to know that this is not all in code?' he demanded, with a triumphant glint in his eye.

Despite her fears, Betty was unable to suppress her exasperation. 'My dear man. If we had valuable coded intelligence in our possession, do you really imagine we'd wrap up our food with it?'

The German's jaw dropped and for a moment he looked abashed. The other Germans were looking at him quizically, but he was not going to admit that he had made a fool of himself. He started to bluster. 'You Italians are all the same, but why should we care any longer whether you are spies as well as traitors?'

Tearing the offending sheet of paper in half, he gave vent to the rage that had been boiling up inside him, caused by the humiliating situation in which he, as a member of the master race, now unaccountably found himself.

He turned on Betty, the latest instrument of that humiliation: 'You wait, my fine Signora. You wait until you have been raped by an American nigger. Oh yes, that's what they are doing, your gallant liberators. You will wish then that you hadn't cheered on Badoglio when he stabbed his German allies in the back.'

Meanwhile the other Germans, weary of this sterile political confrontation, had resumed their search for loot. They threw the food of both families on to a blanket. Then one of them tied the four corners and pitched the bundle over his shoulder.

This was too much for Alec. 'Hey, that's all the food we've got.'

Betty hissed frantically: 'For goodness sake keep your mouth shut. Do you want to get us all shot?'

The Germans had, however, lost interest in the inhabitants of the barn and were already on their way, leaving behind utter chaos, no food and several frightened children. Graziella and Fiorella were crying and clinging to their mother, while Teresa was standing in the middle of the barn bawling, probably mainly because of the stolen chocolate.

All the village activities now went on at night. In the evenings, after the women and animals had come down from the woods and the few mostly elderly men had returned from jobs in Spoleto, everyone would meet in the village square. They knew there would be no more raids until daylight, for no German or fascist would venture on the steep and narrow path from Spoleto in the dark, so they were safe till morning. Bread was baked, meals were prepared and eaten and everyone relaxed as they chatted by candlelight over the day's happenings. With strong verbal support from his indefatigable old mother, Raffo made sure that rations were provided for Betty and the children and for any other inhabitants who had been unable to hide their food stores before the Germans started to loot the village.

Two days later Raffo returned from work early in the afternoon with the exciting news that several German detachments had passed through Spoleto heading north. 'It looks as if the Allies are on the move again.'

The boys asked Betty if they should start loading up the handcart.

'Better wait till we're sure the Germans have all gone.'

Next morning being Sunday, Raffo and most of the other men went up to the woods to collect fuel for the wood-burning stoves used for cooking. About midday Betty heard a commotion and ran out of the barn, fearing another raid by Germans or fascists.

This time, however, the boot was on the other foot. Three or four bedraggled figures in German uniforms were being dragged into the village, none too gently, by Raffo and his friends, while an aged *contadino*, armed with a long sharpened stave like a pike, prodded them on from behind.

When the women saw their hated enemies, they crowded round, screaming and spitting. Betty, anticipating a possible lynching, pushed her way through the throng and put herself between the dejected captives and the infuriated women, one of whom shouted: 'What have you done with our food, you greedy swine? Eaten it all?'

Betty asked Raffo where he had found them.

'Skulking in the woods.'

'If they took part in the raid, I wonder why they didn't make off afterwards with the other Germans.'

Raffo shrugged.

One of the soldiers looked up at Betty with a woebegone expression.

'*Scusi, Signora. Posso explicare*?'

'You speak Italian, then.'

A glimmer of hope appeared in the man's eyes. 'A little, Signora. Please tell these people that we are not Germans.'

Betty looked at their German uniforms. 'What are you, then?'

'Poles and Czechs. We were pressed into the German army when they occupied our countries.'

'What were you doing in those woods?'

'We were with the Germans who raided this village, but when they split up to search the houses we took the opportunity to desert. We've been hiding in the woods ever since.'

This revelation evoked cries of astonishment. The whole atmosphere changed. Amidst murmurs of '*Poveretti*!' from the soft-hearted women, the soldiers were plied with the villagers' scarce and precious wine and invited to share their midday meal.

Early next morning the village was awoken by the boom af an explosion. They all dashed to the highest vantage point, from which they could see right across the vale of Spoleto. They could hear more explosions as the retreating Germans blew up one of the principal gateways to the town, Porta Garibaldi, the munitions factory and what was left of the station. Fires could be seen at various places around the town and across the valley.

They were all crazy with excitement. It took very little time to pack up their sadly diminished baggage and load it on to the handcart. After emotional farewells to the villagers and special hugs for old Emilia and their dear friend Raffo, they set off for home.

It was all downhill, excitement leant wings to their feet and at one point the handcart nearly ran away with them. In no time Colle Attivoli and Casa San Marzano came into view below them. Whooping with joy, they bowled through the front gate into the courtyard.

Standing before the front door, bristling with arms, stood three villanous-looking men.

PART IV
Bandits and Liberators

As the handcart rattled to a halt, the men turned, their fingers reaching instinctively for their weapons. Piratical though they looked, with brightly coloured scarves knotted round their necks and several days' growth of beard, at least they were not wearing fascist black shirts or carrying whips.

One of them addressed himself to Betty. 'Are you Signora di San Marzano?'

She nodded.

'Then you must come with us immediately. Capitano Fondacaro, our leader, has taken over Spoleto and he commands your presence.'

Betty's experience with the Germans and the fascists had taught her that it was always worth resisting peremptory demands and playing for time. She looked steadfastly at the man who had spoken. 'I'm afraid I can't do that. As you can see, I have only this moment returned from hiding in the hills. I have my house to put in order and my family to look after.'

The man frowned. 'Your own affairs will have to wait, Signora. Capitano Fondacaro is not a patient man.' The other two nodded assent.

Betty smoothed a hand down her crumpled dress. 'Look, I have been living and sleeping in these clothes for the last week. I am sure *il Capitano* would like me to be looking my best when I meet him. Will you return in three or four hours?'

All three men shook their heads vigorously. Clearly, they had no intention of letting their quarry escape just when it had appeared so providentially.

Betty sighed. 'Well, you'll have to wait while I change.' Before they could protest or bar her way, she walked quickly into the house. The children followed her and she told Enrico to find Serafina, who would have to look after them while she was gone.

As she washed and put on fresh clothes Betty tried to remember what she had heard about Fondacaro, whose name was familiar to her. She had an idea that he had an unsavoury reputation, but for what she could not recall.

'I expect I'll soon be back,' she told the children as cheerfully as she could. 'Meanwhile, you'd better unload the cart and sort out our things.'

At least feeling cleaner and more presentable, she allowed herself to be escorted down to the town and into the presence of Capitano Fondacaro.

He was small and dark. Though slightly hunchbacked, he seemed to exude vitality. Kissing Betty's hand and bowing low, he said: 'Ah, Contessa, it is a great pleasure to meet you. I hope you will help me to govern this town until the Allies arrive.'

Glancing round at the fierce uncompromising faces of his bodyguard, Betty realised that there was no point in refusing. 'What would you require me to do, Capitano?'

Fondacaro beamed. 'I badly need an assistant whom I can trust, Contessa. Most of the educated people of Spoleto are in some way implicated with the old regime and I refuse to have anything to do with them. After all, my little band of patriots and I have been fighting the enemy in the hills while you, I hear, were vilely threatened by the cowardly fascists who have fled to escape your vengeance.'

'How long have you been running the town, Capitano?'

'We joined other partisan bands in harrying the enemy when he started to withdraw. Then we swooped down from the hills and took over.' Fondacaro made a gesture like a swooping hawk. 'As you doubtless know, the Germans evacuated the town in a great hurry. They left behind utter chaos and disruption. The people were desperate. "Capitano, we shall all starve," they told me. "Trust me and my brave comrades," I answered. "We shall see that you come to no harm." And we have kept our promise, haven't we, lads?'

He looked round for confirmation of this claim from his henchmen, who leered and nodded.

'Yes, Contessa,' he went on, 'we have done everything we possibly could in such a short time to restore normality, in spite of almost overwhelming difficulties. I have requisitioned vehicles and petrol so as to get transport back on the road and bring in the foodstuffs they must have if they are not to perish. I have enabled shops to reopen and firms to start trading again. You will be able to tell the Allies about my efforts when they arrive, Contessa.'

Betty began to see light. 'He wants to hold me as a hostage in case the Allies don't take such a favourable view of his activities as he does himself,' she thought. Later, however, she had to admit that some of his claims were justified and that the Fondacaro inter-regnum was about the best that could have been hoped for at the time.

Betty was called for each morning and often taken round by the partisans to 'supervise' shops, standing by helplessly while they 'requisitioned' whatever they fancied. At lunchtime she was accompanied home, sometimes with parcels of food to feed the family. She received no pay, of course, so felt justified in accepting anything that came her way without looking too deeply into its source.

In the afternoons they drove out into the country in two or three cars, visiting farms and outlying villas. Here Fondacaro showed his true colours, arresting anyone who might conceivably be suspected of collaboration with the Germans or fascists and appropriating what he wanted.

He was usually accompanied by his mistress, a handsome but taciturn woman called Lilla, from northern Italy. Seated side by side with Lilla in the back of Fondacaro's car, Betty made some feeble attempts at light conversation, but these evoked no response so they sat in complete silence. Lilla was on edge all the time, by no means the glamour girl one would have imagined as a bandit's paramour. Betty never found out how she fitted into the picture or where Fondacaro had acquired her.

'I hear you've got a new job, Betty,' said Angelina de Marchis, who had come to supper at Casa San Marzano. 'What is it?'

'I'm Personal Assistant to a bandit.'

'Oh well, better than being a gangster's moll, I suppose.'

Betty grinned. 'That post is already occupied.'

By now everyone was sure that the Allies could arrive at any moment and the mood of expectancy became feverish. Resigned to the end of his reign in the very near future, Fondacaro became more and more active, but also increasingly honest so as to be able to appear as the hero and saviour of the town.

'I sometimes think the people don't appreciate how much I have done for them, Contessa,' he complained.

Betty could safely agree.

Betty was sitting in Capitano Fondacaro's office when the door was flung open and a young man burst in, flushed with excitement.

'The Allies have taken Terni. They're certain to be here today.'

Fondacaro got to his feet, looking grave. 'How do you know, boy?'

'My brother works in Terni. He saw the Allies enter the town, then leapt straight on his bicycle and pedalled over here to let us know the great news.'

'We are fully prepared to welcome them.' Nevertheless Fondacaro had turned pale. He waved a hand towards Betty. 'This is my Personal Assistant and interpreter, Contessa di San Marzano, who is English and will be able to tell our comrades-in-arms how hard we have worked to restore normality to this town.'

The young man looked at Betty with interest. 'Which do you think will arrive here first, Signora? The tanks? Or perhaps the big guns, so that they can shell the Germans as they retreat to Foligno?'

'I'm afraid the Allies haven't told me their order of battle,' Betty answered, sorry to disappoint him.

In Italy news spreads faster than anywhere in the world and within minutes almost the entire population of Spoleto had gathered in the Piazza. A notable absentee, however, was Capitano Fondacaro.

A sudden hush descended on the chattering crowd as the sound of an approaching vehicle was heard and a moment later a British jeep swept into the Piazza. The crowd gave a ragged cheer. The excitement reached its peak as the passenger door of the jeep opened and a most immaculate lieutenant stepped out. The mystified people of Spoleto, who had expected at least a contingent of troops to take over their town, rushed forward and gathered round the solitary vehicle which apparently represented the Allied armies. Betty was, of course, pushed forward to act as their spokesman.

'Who are you?' she asked.

The lieutenant, who had been scanning a document which he was holding daintily between forefinger and thumb, replied in exquisitely modulated tones:

'I am Fine Arts and Monuments. What a relief to find someone who speaks English! I'm afraid my poor little bit of Italian is totally inadequate and the Umbrian dialect is too awful for words.'

Betty was so astounded by this speech that all she could do was to assure the lieutenant that he was most welcome. Meanwhile several people were whispering impatiently into her ear, demanding to know what the English officer had said. Shaking herself free, she asked the lieutenant what his mission in Spoleto might be.

'I have come to discover the whereabouts of certain pictures and works of art which used to be in the gallery here,' he said. Then, lowering his voice to what was intended to be a confidential whisper, he added: 'My dear, I'm told – mind you, one can't take anything on trust these days – I'm told you have a Madonna and Child of Lo Spagna. Do put me out of my misery. Is that true?'

Betty was beginning to enjoy herself. 'It certainly was here, but I believe all the pictures are stored in the cellars of the town hall.'

The lieutenant looked as if he might cry. 'Oh what a bore! I was so looking forward to seeing it, but the light in a cellar would be impossible, wouldn't it?'

Betty felt she must try to cheer him up. 'You could see the frescoes of Filippo Lippi in the Cathedral.'

He gave a whinny of joy. 'Fillipo Lippi! One of my very favourite Italian masters. What an unexpected bonus! Do lead me to them straight away. I can't wait.'

With the population of Spoleto following in what looked like a huge procession, Betty led the way to the Cathedral. The lieutenant chatted politely to her about the works of art that had most impressed him during his campaign, apparently oblivious of the wondering multitude following at their heels. On emerging from the Duomo he noted down the information he had gleaned in his notebook.

Then the Liberator of Spoleto swept on northwards in hot pursuit of the retreating Germans, whence distant firing could be heard.

There was no further sign of the Allies until next day, when a small truck stopped in the Piazza and a figure wearing the insignia of a colonel descended. Dignified, portly and middle-aged, he could not have been anything but English. Again everyone gathered round, while expectant eyes peered down the Rome road to see if the occupying force was arriving. But the colonel too was quite alone, and his reply to Betty's inquiry as to his identity was even more astonishing.

'I am the liaison between the Roman Catholic and the Protestant Churches. I would like to see the Archbishop.'

Spoleto, being one of the biggest dioceses in Italy, had its own archbishop. Among the throng in the Piazza were several priests and Betty asked one of them to accompany the colonel to the Archbishop's palace.

Perhaps the priorities were right, Betty pondered as she lay in bed that night. Spiritual values came first, and Religion and Art were more important than the paraphernalia of War.

Spoleto again found itself without any administration, as it had been when the Germans first pulled out. No car was sent for Betty next morning. She walked down to the town, but when she looked into Fondacaro's headquarters, in an office off the Piazza, it was empty

Eventually she ran across the Capitano slumped in a chair outside a café and staring gloomily at an untouched glass of wine. His manners as well as his normal ebullience had deserted him, for when he saw Betty he made only a token gesture of getting to his feet before waving her to a chair beside him.

'What's happened, Capitano?' Betty asked. 'Have we been given the sack?'

Fondacaro frowned. 'Why don't the Allies get on with it, Contessa? What do they think they are doing, sending in dilettanti dressed up in officers' uniforms to ask silly questions about art and religion? What do art and religion matter at a time of crisis like this?'

Or at any other time, his tone implied.

'Perhaps you will have to take over again, Capitano.'

Fondacaro thumped his hand on the table, upsetting some of his wine. 'Impossible! The people of this town have turned into a hysterical rabble. Only the iron fist of the military could bring them to their senses, but all the Allies send are a pansy and a priest in uniform. What could a patriotic civilian like me do? No, Contessa, I intend to leave them to stew in their own juice.'

Betty guessed that if the Allies were not on the point of occupying the town, Fondacaro would be showing his own iron fist in no uncertain manner. She left him and returned to the Piazza, still crowded with expectant citizens. Just as she got there a truck with two supporting jeeps drew up on the other side of the square.

The British Captain who got out of the truck was greeted with slightly less enthusiasm than the first two liberators. After all, he might turn out to be in charge of recreational activities or something equally important, Betty thought.

However, he waved a hand for silence and announced, in quite good Italian, that he was the Civil Affairs Officer representing A.M.G. (Allied Military Government) and had been sent to take over the town. This statement was cheered loudly by the townsfolk, who hoped fervently that Allied occupation would at last bring them law and order, and above all sufficient rations. What had not been swiped by the Germans and Fondacaro's 'partisans' was hidden away ready to sell at inflated prices to the Allies. But the civilian population, long accustomed to deprivation, felt that at any rate things could not be any worse, and they hoped for a better deal.

The British Captain had, of course, been told at once about Spoleto's most valued and now most prestigious citizen, the English Contessa, and Betty was escorted proudly through the crowd to be introduced.

'I'm Bernard Jay,' he said. 'I'm delighted to meet you.'

'Not half as delighted as we are to welcome you,' Betty assured him.

'My first official act, if you are willing, Contessa, is to appoint you as my interpreter.'

'I'm Betty Marzano, please. I agree of course, especially if the job is paid, but your Italian sounded very good.'

'Not as good as yours, I'm sure. Let me introduce you to the rest of us. This is Vince, my second-in-command.'

An American lieutenant saluted, smiled and said 'Pleased to know you, Betty. This tall skinny guy is Tony, my driver, and the boys over there will surely introduce themselves as soon as they get the chance.'

There was a chorus of 'Hi-ya, Betty' from Tony and half a dozen other G.I.s. Waving back at them, Betty suddenly felt happier than at any time since the day of the Italian Armistice.

The mechanics of the take-over were interesting. Captain Jay asked to be conducted to the town hall, where he requisitioned two of the large halls and a couple of smaller rooms for his headquarters. The first night they all slept at the local hotel, but next morning the Civil Affairs Officer summoned the ex-Mayor.

'What was he called here, *Podesta* or *Sindaco*?' he asked Betty.

'As you probably know, *Podesta* is the fascist term. When the fascist Mayor, or rather *Podesta*, fled north some weeks after the Armistice, they appointed another one, but to show they were no longer fascists they called him *Sindaco*, from the days before Mussolini. The new chap had been a fascist too of course, but not such a militant one as my old enemy *Podesta* Matafia.'

She told Bernard Jay of Matafia's threat to have them all strung up from lamp-posts.

'Well, we won't confirm his successor in the post anyway,' he said as the ex-*Sindaco* was announced.

Bernard wasted no time on courtesies. 'Please tell him, Betty, to find me a large and comfortable house for myself and my staff. A car must be put at my disposal, with a local driver.'

The ex-*Sindaco* nodded nervously as Betty translated.

'Has he got that? Right. Now tell him to call the heads of all the political parties to a meeting, when they can be rounded up, so that we can choose a new Mayor.'

The ex-*Sindaco* looked a trifle crestfallen, but he had probably not seriously expected to retain his job under A.M.G.

There were political parties of every shade, from true blue to bright red, with assorted types representing them – tall, bespectacled and intellectual; fat and arrogant; small and cunning. Betty was rather attracted to the Communist, vague and artistic-looking, with a flowing black bow at his neck.

They sat round discussing various aspects of the town's administration, not always very clear to Bernard, whose sound knowledge of Italian was impaired by his unfamiliarity with the Spoletan dialect. The candidates were mostly tradesmen, with the odd lawyer, doctor or teacher. Finally Bernard wound up the meeting, promising to let them know next day his decision as to who would be *Sindaco*, a position of great influence and prestige.

'It's going to be a tricky decision, Betty,' Bernard said when they had gone. 'I know I missed quite a lot of what they were saying, but I probably wouldn't understand all the political implications anyway.'

'Several of their parties' policies seemed to me to overlap.'

Bernard laughed. 'Politicians' promises are doubtless much the same the world over.'

But the nine candidates had gone off each one buoyed up by the hope that he might be chosen. They evidently considered that the Contessa was the person best able to influence the British Captain's choice because during the day several bribes, in the form of presents, arrived at the Casa. First came a small car bringing two large and delicious hams – something Betty had not seen for years; later a truck bearing crates of wines and soft drinks; and finally a cart with fruit and vegetables of all sorts. It cut Betty to the heart to have to refuse all these mouth-watering gifts, which would have helped so much to feed her hungry family, but she thought it unfair to favour any one party until Bernard had made his decision.

After further cogitation and discussion next morning he chose the Republican Party candidate, de Filippi, the wine and soft drinks merchant. De Filippi proved quite a good *Sindaco*, impartial and enterprising. He and his council did much to restore trade and, by pushing the police back to normal working, to return some law and order to the town.

A large palace was requisitioned for A.M.G. Luckily, the owners, the Marignoli family, were living in Rome and gave their consent for it to be used. Their own servants ran the house, doubtless with instructions to keep an eye on some of the beautiful objects which had been left out for use. Bernard and his staff must have rattled about in such an immense building, but soon the troops began to arrive and a certain amount of social life sprang up.

A Guards regiment was the first, out from the front line for a rest, then an Indian ambulance corps. Most of them were camped outside the town, though some of the officers were billeted with families. Soon the place was seething with khaki uniforms and the local girls, after years of boredom and austerity, became animated and excited as social functions got going. These were mainly dances, to which the girls had to be escorted by mothers or young brothers as chaperones.

Spoleto had a town band, enthusiastic but not always in tune. When it struck up at the opening ball of the season, in Palazzo Marignoli, Bernard, as host, stepped forward and handed Betty on to the floor, murmuring 'Come on, we'd better start the ball rolling. Oh dear, what an awful pun!'

Suddenly, as they danced alone round the huge ballroom with all eyes upon them, they realised to their horror that the band was giving a Spoleto rendering of 'God Save the King'. They froze to attention in the middle of the room, though probably most of the guests did not know the National Anthem and wondered what it was all about.

The schools were still shut, and as the normal summer holidays in Italy last from June to early October, there had been no reason to do anything about reopening them. In fact the vacant buildings were useful for billets or offices for the various units.

But as the children of Spoleto had been hanging about for months and were getting bored and unruly, the arrival of the troops provided for many roaming youngsters tempting opportunities for petty pilfering and competition in who could be the greatest nuisance. Betty was determined that hers should have something definite to occupy them. Teresa was of course below school age anyway and was happy playing at the Casa with Clelia and the little Sabatini girls, looked after by Olga.

When a Y.M.C.A. rolled into the town and took over a café in the Corso, Betty approached the elderly man in charge. 'I wonder if I could send my son Enrico to help you.'

'Is he bilingual?'

'Oh yes.'

'Just the chap we need. Would you ask him to bring two or three Italian helpers, including a woman to cope in the kitchen.'

So there was her eldest placed in his first job and, Betty hoped, kept out of mischief.

Next day she heard that a small South African unit had arrived and was seeking an interpreter. She sent them Alec, who was immediately dispatched in a jeep with a couple of N.C.O.s to obtain wine, stores, oil and anything else they could find for the mess.

'It's a super job, Mummy,' he said that evening, and Betty had no trouble getting him up next morning. So her second son was now usefully employed and happy.

When she got to her office she found an acquaintance called Annie Marcelli, an Italian-American girl born in New Mexico, waiting to see her.

'I heard you were in charge of A.M.G. Headquarters, Betty.'

'Of the office side, yes, but I haven't got it properly organised yet.'

'I'd be more than willing to help you. I'm familiar with office work. Also,' Annie added with a smile, 'I speak American.'

'Your credentials sound impeccable,' said Betty, engaging her on the spot. She was very pretty and the number of male visitors to Headquarters increased noticeably, though Betty herself had never lacked for would-be helpers.

A girl called Carla also offered her services. She was a good typist and Betty put her in charge of the Pass Office on the first floor. No traffic except Army vehicles was allowed on the roads unless the driver held a pass, either to travel in W.D. vehicles or, with a special order for petrol and a travelling permit, in his own car.

Everyone wanted to get around again, firstly for business or professional purposes, and secondly from a purely personal desire to learn how families, not seen for years, were faring. Parents, husbands, wives, children and even old aunts and uncles living in other parts of Italy longed to see each other again. The Office issued passes in cases of absolute necessity, and for journeys for the common good, such as for getting in essential foodstuffs, but even then a great many questions had to be answered before the pass was issued. Relatives would have to wait until the roads were clearer and not being used for moving troops. That did not stop the relatives from besieging the Pass Office and imploring Carla to issue passes for all sorts of spurious reasons. The number of next-of-kin who suddenly fell dangerously ill in distant parts of Italy was astonishing.

Betty appointed little Billy as messenger boy to run up and down stairs between her office and the Pass Office. Everyone made a fuss of him and he felt very important. So all three boys were now usefully, if not gainfully, employed.

Meanwhile Fondacaro was lying low, watching to see 'how the cookie crumbles', as Vince put it.

'Keep an eye on the fellow,' Bernard Jay told his Military Police Sergeant. 'I don't trust him. Has he handed in his arms yet?'

'No, Sir.'

'Well, tell him that if they're not brought in here by nine o'clock tomorrow morning we'll search their houses, confiscate their arms and run him and his gang out of town.'

'Very good, Sir. May I take the Countess to interpret that?'

'I'd rather not if you don't mind, Sergeant,' Betty said. Fondacaro had, on the whole, treated her with consideration and she did not want him to think that this peremptory order emanated from her. 'You can take Enrico, if the Y.M.C.A. can spare him.'

'I could tell him,' said Billy, who was in the office and listening, agog.

'Not this time, darling, thank you. I need you here.' For Fondacaro to be told to hand in his arms by a child of eight would be the ultimate insult, Betty reflected.

That evening two of the partisans arrived at A.M.G. Headquarters carrying about a dozen rifles and shotguns, rather fewer, Betty thought, than they had had at the time when she had been press-ganged into their service.

The Military Police Sergeant scowled at them. 'Where's the ammunition?'

The partisans looked hurt. 'We couldn't carry it all at once, Sergente.'

'Well, go back and fetch it here *pronto*.'

'*Subito*, Sergente.' The offended men shuffled out, shaking their heads.

Next morning Fondacaro himself appeared and invited the *Governatore*, as he was already universally called, to take a glass of wine with him at the café patronised by the Capitano. Bernard Jay looked none too pleased.

'Tell him I'm very busy, Betty. I'll try to look in there before lunch.'

Betty translated, toning down the brusqueness a little.

'Bloody cheek!' Bernard burst out when Fondacaro had gone. 'What's the rogue up to, I wonder?'

To find out he decided to go to the café, where he found Fondacaro with some of his henchmen. After drinks had been served and the usual pleasantries exchanged Fondacaro sprang some surprising news on Bernard.

'Signor *Governatore*, I am organising a little ceremony in the theatre formally to welcome the Allies and to hand over the keys of the city to you, their esteemed representative.'

The Civil Affairs Officer was so taken aback that all he could think of to say was 'I see'. As soon as he decently could, he made some excuse and left.

'I suppose there's no harm in it,' he said rather gloomily to Betty after lunch.

'Fondacaro didn't do too bad a job before you arrived,' Betty pointed out, 'if one overlooks questionable annexations of persons and property.'

'I don't propose to overlook them entirely.'

'He did produce some order out of chaos just when we needed it.'

'Like Mussolini. He made the trains run to time, didn't he?'

'Oh, I'm not saying Fondacaro wouldn't be a ruthless and corrupt dictator too, if he ever got the chance.'

'I don't fancy hobnobbing with the ruffian in public, but I suppose there ought to be some official handing over of power. It's the sort of thing that A.M.G. approves of. Looks good in a report. "Friendly co-operation with the local people – furthering the spread of democracy" – you know the sort of guff.'

The Spoleto theatre is charming and much admired. It had been closed since the war. Now it was opened up and cleaned, carpets were laid along the aisle and pot plants and aspidistras banked on the stage. Everyone was cordially invited and Fondacaro had made sure that the occasion was well publicised. The townsfolk were none too devoted to Fondacaro, but in Italy a public ceremony is irresistible and many people turned up, as also did some of the troops, out of curiosity.

On the stage, chairs had been placed for the A.M.G. officials, with Bernard, Vince and Betty in the centre of the front row, for commanders of the military units stationed in or round the town – none of whom turned up – for the head of the Y.M.C.A., the *Sindaco* and other party leaders and dignitaries.

'I ought not to be up there,' Betty said when told of the seating arrangements. 'I'm only an interpreter, after all.'

Bernard dissented. 'You're a highly respected citizen and your presence among us inspires confidence. You're a member of the establishment now, Betty, and you'll have to get used to it.'

Proceedings were opened by the band, which played the Italian National Anthem, 'God Save the King', 'The Star-Spangled Banner' and finally 'The Internationale', to the perceptible disgust of the Civil Affairs Officer, while several of Fondacaro's henchmen stood around in picturesque fancy costumes.

Fondacaro himself, smartly dressed in black with a red shirt, introduced the *Sindaco*, who thanked the people for their co-operation in restoring law and order and relative normality to the town. He then paid tribute to the *Governatore* for his 'wise decisions' (particularly his choice of the new Mayor, he implied), for restoring full and unfettered democracy (polite cheers from the other party leaders), and for his efficient and fair administration.

'Finally,' the *Sindaco* concluded, 'I must convey the heartfelt gratitude of us all to the gallant Allied forces, many of whom have sacrificed their lives in order to deliver us, not only from brutal German occupation and the foul, corrupt Mussolini regime, but also from usurpers intent on seizing what little was left to us by the Germans and fascists.'

There was no doubt about the target of this unexpected shaft. But after a quick frown as the *Sindaco*'s arrow found its mark, Fondacaro smiled benignly and joined in the general applause. Clearly, he was not going to allow his beautiful ceremony to be spoilt by an ungrateful creature biting the hand that fed him.

Acting quickly to restore the situation, Fondacaro strode to the rostrum and waved for silence.

'Esteemed *Governatore*, dear Contessa, courageous Commanders, comrades and friends,' he began. 'Let me first endorse the *Sindaco*'s eloquent tribute to the Allied armed forces. As a patriot who has himself fought in the hills against the hated Germans and their fascist jackals, I can safely say that I appreciate, perhaps with a deeper understanding than any civilian's, the glorious feats of our comrades-in-arms.

'I must also pay homage to our greatly respected *Governatore*, who has been grappling on our behalf with enormous problems and so far, I fear, with very little help from outside' – this was, of course, a return crack at the *Sindaco*. 'Here I can sympathise with the *Governatore*, for I faced even worse difficulties when it fell upon me to try to restore some semblance of normality after the filthy fascists had fled.'

With a wave towards Betty, Fondacaro went on: 'How daunting these difficulties were, you have only to ask our dear Contessa di San Marzano, who very kindly volunteered to assist me in my vitally important mission' – 'Volunteered, my foot,' thought Betty.

'You, my friends, know as well as I do that the last thing I wanted was to seize power for myself, even less to retain it. I am not an ambitious man and I am delighted to be able to hand over the administration of your beautiful city to the Allied Military Government in the person of our greatly respected *Governatore*. In earnest of this, and as the first of several liberators of Spoleto' – this reference to Fine Arts and Monuments, and Liaison between the Roman Catholic and Protestant Churches, evoked some laughter from the audience – 'I shall now present to the *Governatore* the keys of the city.'

From a suitcase which Fondacaro had put beside his chair he produced two enormous keys. Seeing these, the audience started laughing and clapping and one wag shouted *'Le chiavi di San Pietro'* ('The keys of St. Peter').

Bernard Jay staggered to his feet to receive the keys, but before he could even stretch out his hand he found himself enveloped in a bear-hug embrace while Fondacaro planted a wet kiss, first on one cheek and then, as he struggled in vain to free himself, on the other. This *coup de théâtre* produced rapturous applause from the audience, who probably thought that the red flush of shame and fury which suffused Bernard's features was caused by deep emotion and gratitude for such a loving gesture.

Speechless, Bernard tottered back to his chair, the huge keys jangling in his hand. Determined to get its money's worth, the audience started calling for the *Governatore*. Still trembling with anger, Bernard took some time to realise this. When he did he whispered to Betty: 'Tell them I'm not bloody well speaking. Tell them to piss off home.'

To more rapturous applause, Betty rose to her feet. 'The *Governatore* has asked me to thank you all for coming here today. He asks you to excuse him if he does not reply to the eloquent speeches which we have heard, though he is greatly moved and gratified by what has been said. He is unaccustomed to public speaking, especially in a foreign language. He has asked me to wish you all well and to close the meeting.'

Still seething, Bernard returned to his office. 'Get his documents. I suspect he's one of the riff-raff who escaped from prison. I'm not going to have him at large, commanding his own following. We'll put Intelligence on to him.'

In a few days they had Fondacaro's complete dossier. Bernard was right: he had escaped from prison. He was a notorious con-man, unscrupulous enough to commit any crime to gain his own ends. Bernard at once had him arrested and put in the Rocca, the old fortress, on what charge Betty did not know.

Next day Lilla, Fondacaro's taciturn mistress, came to see Betty. Her customary edginess had turned to inarticulate desperation and her dark eyes were full of bitterness and rancour. 'He wants to see you.'

'I'm afraid there's nothing I can do for him,' Betty answered. 'I'm only the interpreter here, you know.'

Lilla shrugged. 'I told him as much. I'm off anyway.'

'Oh dear.' Betty thought the woman might at least have stood by Fondacaro in his adversity.

'I never knew he was a convict,' Lilla burst out. 'I believed all his lies, gullible fool that I am. He deserves all he gets.'

'Will you tell him I will come to see him if I'm allowed to.'

'I shan't be seeing him again. I've had enough, thank you. He went on and on at me until I agreed to give you a message, but that's the last thing I intend to do for him, the dirty crook.'

With a toss of her head, Lilla turned and stumped out of the office.

'I suppose I shall have to go and see him, poor wretch,' Betty thought. At that moment Bernard came in with something for her to translate. When she had dealt with it she asked if she could visit Fondacaro in the Rocca.

'What for?'

'It seems he's asking to see me. I don't know why.'

'You're a forgiving woman, Betty. Didn't he more or less kidnap you?'

'Yes, but he didn't treat me too badly, all things considered.'

'All right. I don't know what the visiting hours are at the Rocca, but if you make out a document authorising you to see him at any time convenient to you, I'll sign it.'

Armed with this pass, Betty toiled up the hill to the Rocca. She did not like to ask for A.M.G. transport to visit a bandit in gaol, but she was out of breath when she finally arrived at the castle. The gaoler who opened the big gates looked at her curiously when he learned her business, doubtless contrasting her with Lilla and drawing his own conclusions.

The woebegone figure of Capitano Fondacaro was hunched on a stool when Betty was admitted to his cell, but he perked up a little when he saw her. 'Ah Contessa, I knew I could count on you in my hour of need.'

Betty glanced round the cell, which was sparsely but adequately furnished. A big table in the centre was completely covered with handwritten sheets of paper.

'I'm afraid there's very little I can do for you, Capitano. I'm only an interpreter, you know, but Lilla told me you wanted to see me.'

'Don't talk to me about that woman, please. I made a great mistake when I offered her the hand of friendship.'

Betty tried not to smile at this description of their relationship.

'In fact I have been let down by everyone whom I trusted – except you of course, Contessa. "Put not your trust in princes", says the Good Book, and I should have harkened to it. Even the *Governatore*, whom I was beginning to love like a brother, has disappointed me.'

Recalling the fatal consequences of those brotherly kisses bestowed on the *Governatore* at the theatre ceremony, Betty did not know what to say to this. Pointing to the sheets of paper on the table, she asked whether he was writing his memoirs.

'No, Contessa, I am seeking justice, I am putting the true facts before the authorities.'

'Which particular authorities?'

'First of all, of course, the *Governatore*. I'm certain that some despicable enemy of mine must have borne false evidence against me in order to get me out of the way. Probably a fascist, out to escape retribution for his crimes against the people. I know the *Governatore* is a man of honour who would not intentionally act unjustly, but I fear that in my case, Contessa, he has been deceived.'

To avoid commenting on this, Betty asked to whom the other letters were addressed.

'To the Military Commander in Spoleto – I don't know his name, but I expect you could find out for me. I have also taken the matter higher up. I have always believed in going to the top if one can, don't you agree?'

'What is the top in your case, Capitano?'

'Well, I have written, for instance, to the Allied Commander-in-Chief, General Alexander, and to King George the Sixth.'

Betty goggled. 'May I read what you have written to the King?' she asked.

'Of course, Contessa. In fact I was going to ask you if you would be kind enough to translate my letters to the Military Commander, General Alexander and King George. For all I know they may speak perfect Italian, like our *Governatore*, but it's as well to be on the safe side, isn't it?'

He flipped through the sheets of paper on the table, separating his various letters and eventually passed one to Betty, who read:

'Dearest King Emperor, Your Highness, Majesty,

'As an Italian patriot who, with the valorous comrades-in-arms under his command, fought side by side with Your Majesty's glorious armed forces for the liberation of our beloved country, I am writing to inform your Highness of the terrible and incomprehensible injustice to which I have been subjected following the victorious conclusion of our joint struggle . . .'

When Betty had finished reading the letters and promised to translate and dispatch them, Fondacaro looked much happier. Ever optimistic, he presumably thought that with General Alexander and the King on his side, his incarceration could not last much longer. In fact he languished in gaol until he was handed over to the Italian authorities after they took over from A.M.G. His band melted away and no longer represented any threat to anyone.

The Civil Affairs Officer and his staff settled down to the complex task of restoring normality to town and countryside. Every other day they drove out to isolated villages and farms to tell the inhabitants that they were now under Allied administration and must do their best to help and co-operate for the general well-being.

The A.M.G. contingent was accompanied by an Italian delegation, to make it clear that the regime that would eventually replace the military authorities would be drawn from those already in close and voluntary collaboration with the Allies.

The Italian personnel appointed to assist Bernard Jay were commanded by a Colonel Bruno Mastrangeli, who soon became adept at translating Bernard's 'pep talks', with colourful embellishments of his own. There were also two lieutenants, one of whom manipulated a machine-gun, the barrel of which peeped out of the back of the truck, and two picturesque outriders on motor bikes, one in a pink shirt and the other in what looked like a Napoleonic jacket. This show of force was apparently necessary because there were still pockets of Germans in the hills and woods, though they never saw any.

From the steps of the village hall or the church, Colonel Mastrangeli would call for silence, assure the gathering of their extreme good fortune in enjoying the protection of the victorious Allies, and introduce the Civil Affairs Officer with a protracted eulogy.

This eulogy, though embarrassing to Bernard Jay, enabled him to get straight down to the business in hand. 'There is now no need to hide away foodstuffs or livestock. You can apply for help in the form of farm equipment. Schools should be cleaned ready for use in a few weeks' time. Mines are being re-opened. The Royal Engineers are already repairing the railways, which will be working again very soon. I'm afraid buses and cars cannot be put on the road yet owing to the shortage of petrol.'

This would produce groans from the audience, but Colonel Mastrangeli would hasten to reassure them. 'Don't worry, my friends. The shortage won't last long.'

The Italians are nothing if not lavish in their hospitality, and after the 'pep talk' each village would invariably produce a huge and generous spread for their new overlords – pasta, hams, chickens and delicious, carefully hoarded wines. These banquets generally took place, amidst much merriment, in the open piazza.

Unfortunately, Betty knew, one glass of wine was sufficient for Bernard, who got tight very easily. Being the most important person, he had to keep sober. She decided to let Colonel Mastrangeli and Vince into the secret.

'What shall we do?' she asked them.

'Drink it ourselves,' said Vince promptly. 'We don't want to waste the precious stuff, do we?'

They arranged it so that at the village banquets one of them always sat on Bernard's right and took a big swig from his glass whenever it was refilled. When it was Betty's turn, however, she found that she ended lunch feeling extremely muzzy and liable to drop off to sleep in the afternoon. She tried pouring Bernard's wine into flower pots, if there were any within reach, or on to the ground, if there were not, but it was difficult to do so unobserved, and she took to carrying a small bottle in her handbag.

On one unhappy occasion, however, the seating had been arranged in advance and two of the most attractive village maidens were placed on Bernard's right and left. Betty, Vince and the Italian Colonel watched with horror as the *Governatore*'s glass was replenished over and over again. He started to giggle and make frivolous remarks, urged on by his sycophantic audience. Colonel Mastrangeli, who could bear it no longer, got to his feet and announced that it was time to inspect the village.

The Colonel quickly led the way, followed by Betty, Vince and the local dignitaries. Bernard, weaving, was some way behind. Suddenly, Betty heard high-pitched shrieks and turned round to see what had caused them. Bernard was pursuing the village maidens and pinching their bottoms.

'Oh, well,' said Vince on the way home. 'It's a national pastime, isn't it. When in Rome . . .'

By now Spoleto was full of troops and all sorts of entertainments were being organised to keep them out of trouble and amused when off duty. There was the cinema, of course, and English films were put on. Each unit had its own club or took over a wine shop.

Betty had made friends with the Commanding Officer, a Scot called Bill McPherson, who was a keen amateur artist. One day he confided in her: 'I feel sorry for the men of the Indian Ambulance Unit. There isn't much work for them at present, and they seem to be permanently at a loose end. They don't fraternise, and there's the language difficulty.'

'The Italians tend to be a bit wary of coloured troops,' Betty said. 'It's unfair on the Indians, of course, but the Moroccans have evidently earned themselves quite a reputation for rape and mayhem.'

'They don't drink, so they can't spend their free time in wine shops, like most of our lads do.'

They sat in silence, pondering the problem of how to entertain the Indians.

'I could show them our art treasures,' Betty said at last, 'but I'd need an interpreter.'

Bill sat up with a jerk. 'Wait a minute, I've got an idea. Would you consider drawing the portraits of some of them, Betty?'

'I should be delighted. It would be most interesting.'

Bill arranged for her to go down to the farm where he and two officers on his staff were billeted. He had gathered up about a dozen of the more striking looking Indian N.C.O.s.

Work started amidst much chatter and excitement. They came in to pose, one by one, and she took fifteen to twenty minutes for each. The first three, whom she had drawn full-face, were delighted with their portraits, but soon after she had finished the fourth a tremendous hubbub broke out in the adjoining room. Bill went to investigate and came back roaring with laughter. Betty asked what it was all about.

'You drew the last one side-face, didn't you?'

'Yes. He had such a magnificent profile it seemed a pity not to.'

'When he compared his portrait with the others, he found that he had been given only one eye and one ear. He's most indignant, I'm afraid.'

So Betty had to draw him full-face, like the others, with the requisite number of eyes and ears. This was the beginning of a whole series of snap portraits done by Betty in the town.

As the summer wore on the troops changed, some returning to the front, which was being pushed ever further north, others being sent home for transfer to other theatres of war.

One of the officers billeted in Spoleto said to Betty: 'We never have a chance of meeting Italian girls of good family. They seem to be guarded more closely than a sultan's harem.'

She had heard the same complaint from other officers, so she decided to give small parties for them at the Casa, inviting girls she knew. These proved very popular. They went on picnics and expeditions into the mountains, but, unlike the children, they knew these were only pleasant interludes in a grimmer life.

For the children it was an idyllic season. With most of the adults intensively engaged in putting the town in working order again, they got on with their own lives. Betty's three boys, working as they were with the troops, were somewhat envied by the others, but for them, too, there were plenty of free days and a whole summer to enjoy, with little supervision and no holiday homework. The school books of the fascist regime, with their totalitarian ideology and pictures of Mussolini, had been thrown on a huge bonfire and burnt, as a gesture of liberation.

Endless sunny days of outdoor activity stretched ahead. Inside the palisade the boys and their gang built a log cabin and enlarged the 'encampment' so much that it began to encroach on the garden.

Betty channelled their activities into finding and digging up the box containing their valuables which they had buried. The edge of the vineyard had become overgrown and a lot of hard work went into finding the exact burial site. At last, amid great excitement, it was located and the box disinterred. Apart from the best paintings and silver, many forgotten treasures came to light, including toys and games, but although the box was lead-lined the water had got in and most of the clothes and books were ruined.

When Betty had time she organised a sort of basketball on the *aia*, the large grassy threshing floor outside the gate, or their own version of cricket, adapted to local conditions and those taking part. Left to their own devices, when their parents were occupied, the boys explored the woods and hills, inventing complicated tracking games.

Apart from Enrico and Alec, the nucleus of the gang comprised the de Marchis twins, Nando and Leli, Marcello Cimicchi, the Ciacco boys, combative as ever, and Tonino Mastrangeli, son of the Colonel who accompanied Bernard on his official tours of the countryside. Others came and went, but the gang seemed to grow bigger every day, becoming wilder and more unruly, with an endless stream of yelling boys rampaging through the house and round the garden. The mothers longed for October, when the schools would officially open again and the children would be subject to some sort of discipline.

A separate, quieter group of little girls, Teresa, the Sabatini children and the peasant girls, made houses or played with their dolls in a special corner of the garden.

Betty had long suspected Alec of instigating most of the wickedness in the gang, but she did not expect her suspicions to be so alarmingly and dramatically confirmed. She was relaxing in a deck chair on the terrace, after a tiring day in Spoleto, when she heard a loud bang from the direction of the *aia*, followed by shrieks and screams. She rushed round to the front gate. A girl of about twelve, still screaming lustily, was running down the hill, her hands clasped to one ear. The gang, whose usual din Betty's subconscious had vaguely registered before the explosion, seemed to have melted into the landscape, but Alec, looking extremely shamefaced, was gazing down at a black smoking object smelling strongly of cordite.

'What happened?' Betty demanded.

'It went off.'

‘*What* went off?’

‘Our missile.’

‘Oh my God! Was that girl hit?’

Alec gazed miserably after the receding figure as it disappeared from sight. ‘I don’t know. I don’t think so.’

‘You’d better come inside and tell me exactly what you’ve been up to,’ Betty said grimly.

It transpired that the gang had found some live ammunition on the hillside. By extracting a small quantity of powder from some of the rounds they had succeeded in manufacturing quite a lethal home-made bomb.

‘But we didn’t mean it to go off just when that girl was passing,’ Alec pleaded in extenuation.

His mother glared at him. ‘I should jolly well hope not. You must be mad.’ Alec hung his head. ‘Who is that girl, anyway?’

‘I believe she’s called Rosina.’

‘Where does she live?’

‘Somewhere down the bottom of the hill.’

At that moment there was a thunderous knocking on the front door. Outside Betty found Rosina’s enraged parents, red in the face and out of breath. They looked as if they had run up the hill.

The mother opened the onslaught. ‘Are you aware that a gang of ruffians led by your son has just tried to kill our only child?’

‘I’m desperately sorry,’ Betty said, ‘but I do assure you it was an accident.’

‘An accident, indeed! They waited until our Rosina was passing and then threw a bomb at her. She felt the pieces whistling past her ear.’

‘No one threw anything, Signora. The boys were playing with some live ammunition they had found and it went off by mistake just as your daughter was passing by.’

The father took over. ‘It couldn’t have been ammunition going off. We heard the explosion from our house right down the hill, half way to Spoleto. It must have been a bomb.’

‘Is your daughter hurt, Signora?’

This was too much for Rosina’s mother. ‘Of course she’s hurt. It’s lucky she wasn’t killed.’

‘Where was she wounded, Signora?’

‘She was deafened by the blast. She’ll probably be deaf for life, *poverina*. I ask you, what has she done to deserve this?’

It seemed, then, Betty gathered with relief, that the girl had not in fact been wounded by the ‘missile’.

‘Have you sent for a doctor yet, Signora?’

The woman shook her head. ‘It is intolerable, utterly intolerable. For years and years we are persecuted and tortured by the fascists. Then we are killed and robbed by the Germans. Then the so-called

Allies drop bombs on our heads, and now, when we are supposed to have been "liberated", bands of young delinquents roam the countryside letting off home-made bombs at our children.'

Betty apologised profusely all over again. 'I promise you faithfully it will never happen again. I shall see to that. Meanwhile, I want you to call in our doctor – I'll give you his name and address – and get him to give Rosina a really thorough examination. Naturally, I shall pay his fee, and if you will kindly tell me exactly where you live, I will visit you tomorrow to hear his diagnosis.'

Fortunately, the girl was not hurt at all, only very badly frightened, but Betty felt something would have to be done about Alec. She made enquiries and found that there was a boarding school run by priests at Spello, a small hill town about twenty miles away. Bernard drove her over there and she arranged that Alec should be admitted in the autumn term. This plan was greeted with little enthusiasm by Alec who, however, eventually consented to go, doubtless thinking that the school might provide a new field for adventure.

With great difficulty the necessary school gear was collected – sheets and towels much patched, from the linen cupboard, a drab grey uniform, and odds and ends from all the family. There had been nothing in the shops for years and their wardrobes were almost non-existent.

On the appointed date in late September they went over to Spello and, with a sigh of relief, Betty delivered Alec into the hands of a tall lean priest in a black cassock. He looked very severe, but she thought she detected a twinkle in his eye.

As the big doors clanged shut on a rather forlorn little figure, Betty wondered if she was doing the right thing. Then, remembering the 'missile', she decided she probably was.

Enrico presented no problem. Now in the Upper School, he was glad to return to his studies and some sort of ordered life. His friends came up to the house most afternoons after school and they did their homework together, though Betty never understood how they could concentrate with the radio blaring till late at night.

Billy was sent to the local convent, which was also a primary school. It was a delightful place with a sunny cloister full of plants and flowers where the children played. The nuns looked sweet and kind, though Billy soon found out that they could be as fierce and strict as any male teacher. Languages were also taught, which was unusual in a primary school.

Billy had not been at the school long before the nun who took the English Class asked to speak to Betty.

'I find Billy knows quite a lot of English,' she said, 'but would you please tell him not to correct my pronunciation in front of the whole class. It's rather humiliating!'

Spoleto was almost back to normal. Schools were open, factories functioning, and now that communications were easier the shops were filling up with stock.

A.M.G. was in the process of handing over to the Italian authorities and its task was coming to an end. It was no longer responsible for the run-of-the-mill malpractices and evasion of regulations, but still held occasional 'summary courts' to deal with minor offences, mainly stealing Allied property. The proceedings were held in English and Bernard, a solicitor in private life, knew how to get through them expeditiously.

Betty sometimes found simultaneous translation difficult. No one laughed at what, she would suddenly realise, were decidedly comic pronouncements, but she and Bernard would enjoy them in retrospect.

They reduced the office hours, and this gave Betty more time to deal with her domestic problems. The Pass Office too had less to do, as the Italians, on the rare occasions when they could obtain petrol, were now allowed to move freely on the roads.

Even with the reduced hours, time dragged in the office. Someone found a couple of ping-pong bats in a drawer, and they organised matches against the Pass Office and others, using screwed-up paper for a ball and desks for a net.

One day Betty and Bernard were engaged in a strenuous contest against Annie and Vince when there was a peremptory knock on the door. They scrambled back to their desks and tried to look busy. Bernard shouted 'Come in', and two young naval officers entered.

Spoleto being a long way from the sea, they were surprised to receive a visit from the Royal Navy, but they were even more astonished when one of the lieutenants, after saluting Bernard smartly, said: 'Excuse me, Sir, could you tell us where we can find an English lady called Betty di San Marzano?'

They had been sent from Naples by Admiral Anthony M., an old family friend who knew Betty lived near Spoleto. He was in command there, they explained, trying to get the port working again – a gigantic and daunting task, as the Germans had wrecked everything they could and sunk craft in the harbour prior to their evacuation.

'The Admiral wants to know if there's anything you need.'

Instinctively, Betty said 'No'. Then, realising how far from the truth this was, she laughed. 'If I told him all the things I needed, he'd have a fit.'

The lieutenants themselves looked disconcerted. 'Anyway, the O.C. wants us to take you down to Naples for a few days' holiday.'

Betty could hardly believe her ears. She hadn't had a holiday for years. How wonderful it would be to relax, far from all the problems besetting her! But – she looked wildly at Bernard.

'Of course you must go,' he said. 'Annie and I can easily cope here, can't we, Annie? You know how slack things are now.'

Betty beamed. 'Bless you both!'

The sailors drove her back to the Casa to gather together what rags she had. 'And they are literally rags,' she thought. 'Whatever will Anthony and those smart naval wives think of me?'

She said as much to Olga, who promised to help Serafina look after Billy and Teresa while she was away.

Olga looked her up and down appraisingly, the slim, well-proportioned figure, glistening chestnut hair, cheeks flushed with excitement, eyes sparkling.

'You're so pretty, Betty, no one will notice what you are wearing. I don't know if I ought to let you loose among all those handsome English sailors.'

They reached the outskirts of a blacked-out Naples as dusk was falling. Anthony had taken over a beautiful seventeenth-century palace, an architectural gem of the late Renaissance, just out of the town on a promontory jutting out into the sea, with magnificent views of the Bay and Vesuvius.

Betty walked up the steps of this palace, and into another world, a fantastic forgotten world of luxury, comfort, delicious food, smooth wines and plenty of time in which to enjoy it all.

Anthony greeted her fondly, and when she expressed her admiration of the lovely place that was his temporary home, he said: 'Yes, you know I'm the first resident British admiral since Nelson.'

'You must be tickled pink.'

'I am. What's more, the Commander-in-Chief, who's arriving shortly, is taking over the Villa Emma further along the Bay. That's the villa where Nelson housed Lady Hamilton, of course.'

The Navy had turned the beautiful island of Ischia into a rest and leave centre. Here Anthony and his staff used the German Ambassador's villa. Moreover, whenever they needed a few hours' well-earned relaxation, they could sail over to the island in the *Delfino*, King Victor Emmanuel's yacht, which had been commandeered by the Royal Navy.

Betty had been delighted to learn that Anthony's sister Enid, an old friend and a fellow artist, had come out from England on a holiday and was staying at the villa on Ischia.

'I'm sure I can put you in the way of doing some portraits,' he said, 'starting with myself.'

Enid and Betty were overjoyed to see each other again. They

sketched together every day, and Betty painted portraits of Anthony and the Flag Officer.

The waters round Ischia are thermal and there were two hot springs in the villa's private cove, so even though it was nearly mid-winter they could bathe in caressingly warm water. It was utterly peaceful and dreamlike. All sorts of exotic plants and heady perfumed flowers grew in the grounds, with aromatic herbs underfoot.

By the time this idyllic holiday came to an end Betty felt marvellously refreshed. Kissing her farewell, Anthony said: 'Next time you come you must bring one of your children for a little sea air.'

She returned to Spoleto with lots of food and yards of Navy serge to make clothes for herself and her children.

Soon afterwards came A.M.G.'s official hand-over to the Italian Government, Bernard and his staff having been posted to a town further north. There were several hectic farewell parties, and Bernard himself gave a Reception in his lovely home, Palazzo Marignoli, to which he invited the *Sindaco* and Town Council, the Military Commander and Head of Police, representatives of the Chamber of Commerce, and also some of the wealthy titled landowners who had given them lavish hospitality. It was a very mixed party and some underlying currents of jealousy and hostility could be felt, but all were unanimous in praising Bernard's work, thanking him for what he had done for Spoleto and wishing him well in his next post.

Betty had got to know two young officers of the Royal Engineers, Alan and Douglas, who had been in charge of the repair and running of the railway from Rome. They found a job for Enrico for part of the Christmas holidays as assistant interpreter at the canteen on Terni station. He was allowed to help drive the engine from Terni to Spoleto every evening, arriving home black but exuberant. Alec returned from Spello, not much enamoured of his new school and rather jealous of Enrico's engine-driving feats. There was no snow, as there had been last year, but it rained torrentially. Alan and Douglas helped to enliven Christmas Day but Betty felt that, paradoxically, it was not such fun as Christmas 1943, which the families and children had celebrated on their own, but united in adversity.

'There's a Signor Nalli to see you, Signora,' Serafina announced.

Betty was in the drawing room making a pair of dark blue shorts for Billy out of the naval serge.

'Nalli. Do we know him, Serafina?'

'I don't. And he wouldn't say what he wanted.'

'Oh well, you'd better show him in.'

Signor Nalli was thin and austere looking. He kissed Betty's hand, but did not return her smile. His manner was solemn. 'Signora, I bring you news of Colonello di San Marzano.'

This was the last thing Betty had been expecting, and the man looked so grave that she was gripped by a terrible fear. She could only gasp, 'Is he all right?'

'Oh yes, Signora. At least he certainly was when last seen.'

Betty's heart gave another heave, this time of relief. 'When did you see him, Signor Nalli?'

'I have not seen him personally. The news arrived through certain channels which I am not at liberty to talk about.'

'But where is he?'

'In Turin. I understand he had been fighting with the partisans in the Alps, but as winter set in he found the life too hard and exhausting. Somehow he managed to get back to Turin. He has a room in Via Flavia and is working in a jeweller's shop.'

'Did he send me a message?'

'Yes, Signora, he did. He told us to tell you that as soon as Turin is liberated he will try to get down to Spoleto.'

Betty would have kissed Signor Nalli if he had not looked so forbidding. 'How wonderful! You couldn't have brought me more thrilling news. You must drink to it with me in the best wine I can find.'

'That's very kind of you, but I do not drink, thank you, and I have a lot of matters to attend to. If you have no more questions, I must be going.'

Betty thought frantically. She hated to let go of this tenuous link with Valentino. 'Do you know how long ago my husband gave this message to your informant, Signor Nalli?'

'I'm afraid I do not, Signora. All I can tell you is that the message has been passed by word of mouth from person to person. And now, if you will excuse me – '

Betty could think of no further pretext for detaining him and had to let him go.

Vague though Nalli had been, at least they knew that Valentino was safe and well, though goodness knows how long the message had been on the way. And surely it wouldn't be long before the Germans were pushed out of Italy altogether. She decided that when she next went to Naples she would ask Anthony whether he could help in contacting Valentino, when the situation permitted, and finding transport for him from Turin to Spoleto. Then she dashed out to tell the others the glad news.

The school holidays came to an end and Alec returned reluctantly to the school at Spello. Enrico, who had been unwell, did not go back at the beginning of term, and when Anthony telephoned to say that he was sending for her shortly, she asked if she could bring the boy for a few days' convalescence. It was quite an adventure for him, as he had not been away from home since before the war.

Naples was very cold and there was snow on the hills. Vesuvius had recently erupted and still had a black cap of hardened lava. Now the snow had made white streaks down the volcano parallel with the black streaks of lava that had poured down its sides.

Betty and Valentino had spent their honeymoon in Naples and one of their excursions had been to Vesuvius, where they had climbed down into the crater. Betty had good reason to remember this: she had been jumping excitedly from one piece of lava to the next when a foot had gone through the crust, cutting her leg nearly to the bone. Valentino and the guide had carried her up the side of the crater, the leg had required several stitches and she had had to spend two or three precious days of her honeymoon in bed in their Naples hotel.

These memories recalled Valentino vividly to her, and as soon as she got to the palace and had been welcomed by Anthony, she asked if he could help Valentino to get back to Spoleto when Turin was liberated.

He looked at her a trifle ruefully but then smiled and said, 'Of course I will, my dear.'

Enrico was thrilled with everything and was soon restored to bouncing health. He spent his days with the domestic staff, and the Chief Steward, a tall lanky Cornishman known as Tiny, took him under his wing. He was occupied and happy, boating and exploring Naples. They even kitted him out with a petty officer's uniform and took him with them to the cinema and the NAAFI.

'By the way, Betty,' Anthony told her soon after their arrival, 'the Commander-in-Chief came to dinner here last week. He greatly admired the portrait you did of me on your first visit and he wants you to paint him.'

'Oh golly!' said Betty, her consternation expressing itself in schoolgirl slang.

'It would be purely an informal portrait, of course. His wife, Lady C., is arriving from England soon and he wants to give it to her as a birthday present.'

'If I make a mess of it, you'll probably lose your promotion.'

'You'll like him, I think. He's a nice old buffer, if a bit vague at times. A good sailor too, especially in wartime – he cuts through the red tape – though funnily enough he's not a "good sailor" in the landlubber's sense because he gets seasick very easily.'

'Sounds a bit like *H.M.S. Pinafore*.'

'If it hadn't been for the war he would have retired by now.

Personally, I'm glad he hasn't. Well, Betty, will you do it?'

She wrinkled her nose. 'All right, I'll have a stab at it, if you like.'

Anthony got on the telephone and a sitting was arranged for the next day. Betty was called for, her easel, paints and canvas were piled into the Admiral's big black limousine and she was escorted, with outriders, along the coast road to Villa Emma.

The Admiral greeted her with old-world courtesy and showed her to the stately room that was to serve as a studio. 'Will this do, dear lady?'

Betty gazed admiringly at the beautiful fresco on the ceiling. 'It's lovely, but could we rig up something for you to pose on? A sort of platform, if possible.'

The Admiral went to the door and called: 'Jeavons!'

A smartly turned out petty officer appeared: 'Sir?'

'The lady wants me to sit on a platform. Could you erect one, do you think?'

'I'll do the best I can, Sir.'

'That's a good fellow.' The Admiral turned to Betty: 'Meanwhile, perhaps you'd like to see Lady Hamilton's boudoir.'

When they returned Jeavons was putting the finishing touches to an improvised platform erected by two naval craftsmen. On it stood an ornate gilded chair.

All went well for about twenty minutes, but then Betty looked up and saw that the Admiral had dozed off. His body was slumped in the chair, his jaw had dropped and his mouth was open. She could not possibly go on painting him like that.

She gave a discreet cough. No reaction. She called his name. The Admiral began to snore. She let out what she fondly imagined was a loud nautical hail. The Admiral slumbered on. Desperate, she shouted at the top of her voice: 'Ship ahoy!'

Very slowly the Admiral opened his eyes, very sweetly he smiled at her. 'How are we doing, dear lady?'

'Nicely – now, Admiral, thank you.'

There was a patter of feet outside, the door opened and Jeavons's head appeared. 'Did you call, Madam?'

The Admiral looked at him sternly. 'No one called, Jeavons.'

'I beg your pardon, Sir. I thought I heard someone call "Ship ahoy!"'

'Really! Why on earth should someone call "Ship ahoy" on dry land?'

Jeavons looked as if he might burst into tears. 'I'm sorry, Sir.'

Betty felt mean not to own up, but if she did she would only cause even more embarrassment. Poor Jeavons withdrew, shaking his head.

The Admiral frowned. 'Ship ahoy, indeed! Fellow must be going round the bend. Too long on land, I dare say. Time we put to sea again.'

At breakfast next morning Anthony told Betty that he would shortly be moving north to take over the big port of Livorno.

'What a shame that you have to leave this beautiful palace,' she said, 'to say nothing of the *Delfino* and Ischia.'

Anthony took the impending move philosophically. 'I've been expecting it for some time. Naples is almost back to normal now, and I understand the mess Jerry left behind when he pulled out of Livorno is a whole lot worse than it was here. That reminds me: would you care to take a little jaunt with me today?'

Betty, who was thinking in terms of sea trips, said: 'I'd love to. Where?'

'Well, I've decided to fly up to Livorno to assess the situation for myself. They've requisitioned a villa for me just outside the town, so we could take a look at that, too.'

'How thrilling!'

'The plane they've laid on is only a small one, a Baltimore, I think. You aren't air sick are you, my dear?'

'Never,' said Betty, who had only flown once before in her life.

From Naples they flew right over the crater of Vesuvius, giving Betty a fascinating new perspective of the volcano, and then, making a slight detour, over Spoleto, swooping low over Casa San Marzano. She saw Billy and Teresa waving from the terrace, little knowing their mother was a passenger in the aircraft that came zooming over their heads at tree-top level.

Livorno was a nightmare scene of devastation and destruction, houses reduced to piles of rubble. All the port installations had been blown up, great heaps of twisted metal lying half in the water, sunken craft completely blocking the harbour mouth. Betty wondered how the port could ever be restored to normal.

Having looked over the villa earmarked for Anthony and his staff, they flew back to Naples, where Betty picked up Enrico and her baggage, said a grateful farewell to her host and set off on the journey home to Spoleto.

The morning after her return Betty had just finished breakfast when the telephone rang. She recognised the deep voice of Alec's headmaster.

'I'm sorry to have to tell you that Alec has disappeared. Has he arrived home, Contessa?'

'No, he hasn't.'

'We found his bed empty this morning. We've searched everywhere. I had better tell the police in Spello to keep an eye out for him.'

Betty was not greatly surprised, but felt a trifle anxious. There was no Bernard to call upon for help and transport, but she got one of the young R.E. officers to drive her along the main road towards Spello. There was no sign of the boy, so she returned home. She guessed that Alec had run away from school, as he had told them in no uncertain terms that he did not like it. Confident that he would turn up in due course, she was not unduly worried. The school was, however, and telephoned her at frequent intervals.

Sure enough, late in the afternoon a dirty and exhausted figure toiled up the hill and slumped on to the doorstep in a state of near collapse.

When she had ministered to his needs, Betty asked him if he had walked the whole way from Spello.

'Most of it. I got a lift for a few miles to Foligno.'

'What made you run away?' his mother asked him. 'It's practically the end of the term anyway.'

Alec fought back his tears. 'I hate the beastly place. It's like a prison.'

Betty remembered those huge gates clanging shut and felt a little sympathy for her erring son. 'But couldn't you have stuck it out for the last few days of term?'

He began to sob. 'Why should I? It's not fair. Enrico gets all the fun, driving that engine in the Christmas hols and then going with you to Naples while I'm shut up in that horrid school.'

'Enrico didn't let off that bomb, you know, Alec,' she pointed out.

'He would have been with us if he hadn't been swotting in his room,' Alec retorted indignantly. 'That's another thing that's not fair. He should have got the blame too.'

His mother smiled faintly. 'There's a lot of injustice in the world. It's a lesson we all have to learn.'

There seemed little point in taking him back to the school. He was unhappy there, he missed home and was always in trouble. Next day Betty went over to Spello and told them she was taking him away. They seemed rather relieved. Next term he would return to the Scuola Media in Spoleto, though Betty was aware that he and Marcello had often played truant, going off into the hills for the day.

Betty knew that what Alec needed was his father, and that night she prayed, as she had so often in the past, for her husband's return.

The Almighty must have heard her, for next morning the telephone rang and a blessedly familiar voice said: 'Carissima, I'm on my way home.'

She gasped. 'Valentino! Where are you?'

'Foligno. Your English Admiral helped to spirit me out of Torino, and I got on a train for the last part of the journey. I hope to get a lift to Spoleto almost immediately.'

The boys went mad with excitement and rushed down to the bottom of the hill to meet him. Less than an hour after his telephone call she was in his arms.

Teresa hardly remembered her father, and was embarrassed to be embraced by a strange man, but the boys vied with each other for his attention.

'I was captured by the Fascist Militia,' Enrico said, 'but their Captain knew you and he let me go.'

'I was given a lift by the Germans in a lorry,' Alec said. 'They never guessed I was half English, of course.'

'I took messages from Mummy's office at A.M.G. to the Pass Office,' Billy said, puffing out his chest.

They had a huge celebration supper, and it was midnight before Betty managed to pack the children off to bed. Then, sitting on the sofa with Valentino's arm round her, she gave him a more coherent account of their adventures.

'It's been quite a game,' she concluded.

Valentino smiled at this English understatement and kissed her tenderly.

'It sounds like a game called survival,' he said. 'I'm sorry I was not there to play it with you.'

Epilogue

Over thirty-seven years have gone by since the Italian Armistice and the adventures which it brought in its wake for the family di San Marzano. The youngsters grew up long ago, of course. They all married and had children of their own, but the bizarre and unpredictable game that they found themselves playing with their mother for their survival remains the most vivid and exciting of their childhood memories.

After the war Valentino did welfare work for ex-servicemen for a time, but later he became a professional artist and writer. He died in 1968, aged 72. Many of his evocative pictures today adorn Betty's flat in Hampton-in-Arden, where she now lives.

In view of the difficulties of bringing up her family in Italy amid all the post-war disruption, Betty decided to move to England and to send the three younger children to school there. At first she made her home in Birmingham.

Enrico, who had completed his education in Italy, was determined to join the British Army, but to his consternation he found that he was officially classed as an enemy alien! When proof was provided that his Italian father had joined the partisans after the Italian Armistice and fought on the Allied side, and that his mother was English, the military authorities relented and gave him a commission, first in the Intelligence Corps and then in the Royal Signals.

Enrico, who is now an executive in the international operations of a pharmaceutical company, went to live in Italy in 1975. He also writes poetry which has won him several prizes, including the *Oliva d'Oro* at the Spoleto Festival of 1977 and the international literary prize *Citta di Sagrate* in 1979. He has been married twice and has five children, three by his first wife and two by his second.

Alec is a mechanical engineer. In 1951 he got a job with East Africa Railways and Harbours in what was then the southern province of Tanganyika. As well as working hard, he led a busy social life during which he found himself falling more and more deeply in love with a pretty and vivacious girl called Carol Troup, daughter of the Governor.

There was one small snag, however: Carol was only fourteen years old. Patiently, Alec pursued his courtship. His persistence was rewarded and three years later, when Carol had reached the mature age of seventeen, they were married.

They have four children, aged twenty, eighteen, sixteen and fourteen. Alec now has his own highly efficient engineering works near Doncaster and the family is happy and prosperous.

Billy is an industrial chemist and lives in Singapore. Like Enrico, he has been married twice. He has two boys, aged nineteen and seventeen, by his first wife, and a toddler by his second.

Teresa married an Italian, Aldo Marcocchi, who with his two brothers owned a photographer's shop in Spoleto. Later Aldo became the representative of a furniture firm and they moved to Florence. They had three boys, now aged twenty, seventeen and fourteen.

Betty recalls that the English language sometimes mystified Aldo. One January day soon after they were married, when he and Teresa were visiting her relatives in England for Christmas and the New Year, Aldo asked his wife in Italian why all the shops in Birmingham had suddenly started selling salt.

Teresa looked puzzled. 'Selling salt? What *do* you mean?'

'Haven't you seen all the shop windows?' Aldo asked. 'They've all got labels on them advertising "Sale".'

(*Sale* is, of course, the Italian word for salt.)

Tragically, Teresa's devoted and greatly loved husband died in 1976. She now lives in England near her mother.

In 1958 Betty decided to run the Casa San Marzano as a private *pensione* for four months each summer, and for over twenty years this guest house was her main interest and joy.

'I made so many wonderful friends from all over Great Britain and also from America and Australia,' she says.

This is not surprising, for her guests were offered a highly original holiday of surpassing value. The friendly, comfortable and cultured ambience was appreciated by all, but especially by single, non-Italian-speaking guests who might not otherwise have ventured alone on a holiday in Italy.

Betty organised excursions ranging from the beauty spots and treasures of Umbria to as far afield as Florence and Pompeii. From Spoleto she could call upon the services of two devoted drivers, prepared to act as chauffeurs and also to fetch and carry guests to and from stations and airports. The domestic staff consisted of Clelia, Teresa's boon companion in their childhood, who was an excellent cook, and her sister, Alba.

In the latter years Betty was ably assisted in the catering and administration by a charming retired headmistress, Nora Greenacre, who became a close friend. They invariably did the marketing together every morning. Early waking guests would hear the car leaving the Casa before 7 a.m. and Nora developed a keen eye for the freshest vegetables, the ripest peaches, the most luscious grapes.

Their busiest time came, of course, with the Spoleto Festival in July, when the Casa was always packed with guests, the family being temporarily shifted to a caravan in the garden. Betty would spend most of the day driving her guests to and from the various events of the Festival.

In 1964 she wrote and illustrated a delightful guide to Spoleto.

Betty is now a sprightly 76. She has fifteen grandchildren and one great grandchild, Caroline, granddaughter of Enrico, who was born in Australia in June last year.

In England she plays an active part in local affairs and runs a very popular Art Group in Hampton-in-Arden, but painting still occupies most of her leisure.

In the summer of 1954 Betty came south from Birmingham to shop, see her friends and visit some picture galleries in London. She was staying with her Aunt Olive Brodribb in Knightsbridge.

One evening they were sipping their coffee after dinner when they heard the front door bell ring.

'Who can that be?' asked Aunt Olive. 'I really can't face a visitor like this, in my old housecoat.'

Scrambling hastily to her feet, she made for the door, calling over her shoulder, 'You look after whoever it is, Betty. If I'm needed, call me, dear.'

Meanwhile the maid was opening the front door to the visitor, who was evidently a stranger to her, for Betty could hear her asking what his business might be, and a loud, rather guttural voice replying.

Betty crept across the drawing room and peered out into the hall. Framed in the front doorway was a stout, middle-aged man with a red face.

'It can't be,' she said to herself. 'I must be seeing things.'

The man spoke again, asking if the Contessa di San Marzano was there, and her suspicion became a certainty.

'Emmanuel!' Watched open-mouthed by her aunt's maid, she rushed to greet him.

Grinning broadly, Emmanuel said: 'I promised to come and see you after the war. Remember?'

After Betty had settled him in the drawing room and poured him a large glass of whisky, she asked how he had managed to trace her, and not even at her own address.

'I never forgot my promise,' he answered, 'but after the war I had quite a struggle and for some years I couldn't afford to travel.'

'Are you married?' Betty asked.

'Yes, very happily and I'm doing quite well now. I'm in the tanning trade in Austria. Last year I took my wife on a tour of Italy, including Spoleto, of course. I called at Casa San Marzano, and that Sabatini fellow gave me your address in Birmingham.'

'You still haven't told me how you found me *here*.'

'Well, this year I had to make a business trip to England. I arrived two days ago and got your Birmingham telephone number from – how do you call it?'

'Directory Enquiries. And you spoke to Teresa. Of course!'

'Yes, she gave me your address in London. I got quite a shock to find myself talking to a sophisticated young lady,' Emmanuel went on. 'When I last saw Teresa she was only five or six. Do you remember those drawing books of hers. English, weren't they?'

Betty nodded. 'You suspected all along that we were English, didn't you?'

'Of course, but it was none of my business. All I needed was an Italian house to provide shelter for my men. I wouldn't have cared if you had been Japanese.'

Betty laughed. 'In that case we would have been allies, not enemies.'

'Ah well,' said Emmanuel philosophically, 'we're allies now, aren't we? Let's drink to that!'